SPIRITUAL
WARFARE

SPIRITUAL WARFARE

ATTACK AGAINST THE WOMAN

By
Rev. George W. Kosicki, C.S.B.

*"Lord, we draw strength from You
and Your mighty power."*
Eph. 6:10-20

Faith Publishing Company
Milford, Ohio 45150

Published by Faith Publishing Company

For additional copies write:

Faith Publishing Company
P.O. Box 237
Milford, Ohio 45150

Copyright 1990 Faith Publishing Company

Library of Congress Catalog Card No.: 90-085415

ISBN: 0-9625975-4-6

TABLE OF CONTENTS

DEDICATION

To Our Lady of Guadalupe, the woman of Revelation, who "crushes-the-head-of-the-stone-serpent." May she imprint her image on our hearts.

G.W.K.

INTRODUCTION

"What are the greatest needs of the Church today? Do not let our answer surprise you as being over-simple or even superstitious and unreal: one of the greatest needs is defense from evil which is the devil." (*Paul VI, November 15, 1972, Deliver Us From Evil*).

Pope Paul VI, in this general audience address stirred the post-Vatican II Church with a surprising exhortation. He challenged the Church to study again "the question of the Devil and his influence on individual persons as well as on communities, whole societies or events." Since this exhortation of Pope Paul VI was a major thrust of his pontificate *(See Reference 2)*, I felt the need to respond to his challenge in some small way.

Spiritual Warfare is also an exhortation, echoing the message of "Deliver Us From Evil." The first and most important exhortation is to be aware of the **fact** of spiritual warfare. We **are** in the midst of a cosmic battle. Even if we do not know of its existence or if we ignore it, it does not cease to exist. The fact is we **are** being devastated by the forces of evil, and most do not even know the causes.

This exhortation is also a plea, and a sermon, challenging us to wake up, to snap out of our lethargy, and be conscious of the victory of Christ crucified and risen, and claim it as our own.

To be effective in this battle, we need to know the nature of the warfare and follow the battle plan, using the weapons given us, while being aware of the strategy of the enemy. The victory is ours, but we must take it.

Satan and his forces have blinded this generation to his tactic of secularization. We are so secularized that we don't even know it! This exhortation is an urgent call to counter this secularization of our age.

The intention of this book is to convey the magnificent and wonderful plan for our salvation in Christ Jesus, and the victory which awaits us through our participation in His redemptive Incarnation.

THE BATTLE PRAYER

Adapted from *Ephesians* 6:10-20

Lord, we draw strength from You and Your mighty power.

We put on Your armor so that we may be able to stand firm against the tactics of the devil.

Our battle is not against human forces but against the principalities and powers, the rulers of this world of darkness, the evil spirits in regions above.

We must put on Your armor if we are to resist on the evil day. We must do all that our duty requires, and hold our ground.

So, we stand fast, with *truth* as the belt around our waist, *justice* as our breastplate and *zeal* to propagate the gospel of peace as our footgear.

In our circumstances we hold up *faith* before us as our shield; it will help us extinguish the fiery darts of the evil one. We take the helmet of *salvation* and the sword of the Spirit, Your *Word.*

Lord, at every opportunity we *pray* in the Spirit, using prayers and petitions of every sort. We pray for all in the holy company. We pray for our leaders that You may put Your Word on their lips, that they may courageously make known the mystery for which they are ambassadors, even in chains. We pray that they may have the courage to proclaim it as they ought.

CHAPTER 1

SATAN'S ATTACKS AGAINST SOCIETY AND NATIONS

"...This question of the Devil and the influence he can exert on...whole societies or events, is a very important chapter of Catholic doctrine which is given little evidence today, though it should be studied again..." *(See Reference 1) (Pope Paul VI).*

Satan has power over society, events and nations, because that power has been given him by the Lord God Who created him. But that power has been broken by the death and resurrection of Jesus Christ, and is available to us, the Church, under the leadership of Mary, our Queen. Now we need to take it away from Satan. Herein is the battle. We have the victory in Christ Jesus, but the battle to claim that victory continues in each generation until the day of the coming again of Jesus Christ in His glory. Come Lord Jesus! Come in our day!

The key strategy in Satan's attack against society and nations has been *secularization of mankind.* Gradually, our mind is being reduced into a belief in only the existence of this world which is visible and under man's control. Even the Church and Sacred Scripture have been under attack. Today it comes to us under the guise of new age religion. The Church, in her teachings, does acknowledge the existence of Satan and the fact of spiritual warfare, as we see in the Baptismal Rite. However, this clear teaching of the Church "needs to be studied again" because there is so little awareness of it in the current teachings after the Second Vatican Council. The Council did teach clearly on the influence of Satan in

1

the "Dogmatic Constitution on the Church." *(See Reference 3)*. In speaking of those who do not know the Gospel of Christ or His Church, and still are seeking, the Council said:

> "But rather often men, deceived by the Evil one, have become caught up in futile reasoning and have exchanged the truth of God for a lie, serving the creature rather than the Creator" *(D.C.C. #16)*.

Also, the "Pastoral Constitution on the Church in the Modern World," *(See Reference 4)* the other basic document of the Council, in the preface, teaches:

> "He (Christ) was crucified and rose again to break the stronghold of personified Evil, so that this world might be fashioned anew according to God's design and reach its fulfillment." *(#2)*.

And again, in the chapter on the "Dignity of the Human Person" *(See Reference 4)* the Council teaches:

> "Although he (man) was made by God in a state of holiness, from the very dawn of history man abused his liberty, at the urging of personified Evil. Man set himself against God and sought to have fulfillment apart from God." *(#13)*.

The Synod of Bishops (1985) in its "Final Relatio" spoke of external and internal difficulties since the Second Vatican Council: "We cannot deny the existence in society of forces which act with a certain hostile spirit towards the Church. All of these things manifest the work of the 'prince of this world' and of the 'mystery of iniquity even in our days'" *(#14)*. It also spoke of the changes since the Council, especially in secularism. The Holy Father, at the closing homily on the Solemnity of the Immaculate Conception, quoted the "Pastoral Constitution on the Church in the Modern World," in regard to "personified Evil":

> "Christ was crucified and rose again to break the stranglehold of personified Evil, so that we might be fashioned anew according to God's design and reach its fulfillment."

And further he said,

"Therefore, the Church, the true Church of Christ, experiences that 'emnity' of which the Proto-Gospel *(See Gen.* 3:15) speaks and—through God's grace—has no fear of it."

The message of Our Lady of Fatima, supported by the writing and presence at the shrine of Pope Paul VI and of John Paul II, calls us to be aware of the urgency of the times. Our Lady singles out the Atheist Marxism of Russia, spreading its errors throughout the world. Our Lady also points to the sin of the world, especially the secularization, materialism and impurity. All these are attacks of Satan against society, the nations and the Church. Our Lady has made us aware that we are in spiritual warfare involving nations. She asked for the collegial consecration of Russia to her Immaculate Heart so that the subsequent conversion of Russia will be an honor to her as desired by her Son Jesus. Jesus wants the Immaculate Heart of His mother honored along with His Sacred Heart, and this is the triumph of the Immaculate Heart that Mary speaks of. She will be honored with Jesus, as the head of Satan is crushed by His heel—His Church, the Body of her Son Jesus. This warfare involves nations, societies and kingdoms—and every individual person in them.

The Sacred Scriptures give a very clear picture of the conflict between the kingdom of God and the kingdom of darkness. But the Scriptures, too, are under attack and their teachings on this conflict do not find universal acceptance in our day.

And so it is important to look at Sacred Scripture as it is written, because one of the great deceptions of Satan is to secularize our minds, so that we can rationalize away the very meaning of the words of the Lord. The kingdom of Satan is explained away as meaning that there is no struggle with Satan, but only with the evil in man's heart. Any existence of an adverse Kingdom of darkness and evil is labeled as fundamentalistic and is ignored.

Secularism has progressed greatly in our minds and attitudes, especially during these four centuries since the age of enlightment. These centuries have seen the enthroning of enlightenment in the person of a prostitute in the Cathedral of Notre Dame in Paris; they have seen the rise of deism and an ideology that is militaristic and communistic, and an atheism that is capitalistic and materialistic. This period of history has seen the rise of a scientific and technological society that tries to live independently of God and denies the existence of Satan and his evil spirits.

This is a triumph for Satan. He can go about his roaming and patrolling the earth unhindered (*See Job* 1:6-7). His work is now manifest in widespread atheism, hedonism, militarism and materialism, in one word, *secularism.* Secularism is the full blossoming of Pelagianism, denying original sin and holding that man has perfect freedom of will, and through his own works only can earn his salvation. Secularism is the independent lifestyle that claims to have no need of a God. The fruit of secularism is atheistic communism, which, in a military way, forces its denial of God on others, and a capitalistic atheism that lures man away from God by the goods of this life on earth. Secularism is the temptation of *Genesis* 3: *You will be like gods!*

The Gospel of Luke provides an illustration of the power of Satan over nations, and of how Jesus Christ dealt with this power, inaugurating by His death and resurrection the Kingdom of God, and establishing His Church as the living witness of His reign.

> *When all the people were baptized, and Jesus was at prayer after likewise being baptized, the skies opened and the Holy Spirit descended on him in visible form like a dove. A voice from heaven was heard to say: 'you are my beloved Son. On you my favor rests.' (Lk.* 3:21-22*).*

> *Jesus, full of the Holy Spirit, then returned from the Jordan and was conducted by the Spirit into the desert for forty days, where he was tempted by the devil. . .Then the devil took him up higher and showed him all the kingdoms of the world in*

an instant. He said to him, 'I will give you all
this power and the glory of these kingdoms; the
power has been given to me and I give it to whom-
ever I wish. Prostrate yourself in homage before
me, and it shall all be yours.' In reply, Jesus said
to him, 'Scripture has it, you shall do homage to
the Lord your God; him alone shall you adore.'
(Lk. 4:1-8).

Jesus recognized the power of Satan; He did not deny it,
nor did He submit to it, rather, He confronted it with God's
word. Jesus came in the full power of the Holy Spirit to in-
augurate the kingdom of God—a kingdom of *mercy* to the
poor, the captives, the blind, and prisoners *(See Lk.* 4:18) a kingdom of *power* of the Holy Spirit to deliver sinners and those
under the bondage of Satan *(Cf. Lk.* 4:33-41; 5:12-16;). Jesus had
power that went out from Him as mercy *(See Lk.* 6:19), and He
taught about this merciful kingdom asking us to love even
our enemies and be as merciful as our Father in Heaven is
merciful *(See Lk.* 6:27-36). He also made it clear that those who
follow Him as His disciples are to have authority over the
kingdom of darkness:

Jesus now called the twelve together and gave
them power and authority to overcome all demons
and to cure diseases. He sent them to proclaim the
reign of God and heal the afflicted. (Lk. 9:1-2).

When the seventy-two returned from their mission they re-
joiced that the demons were subject to them in the name
of Jesus.

I watched Satan fall from the sky like lightning.
See what I have done; I have given you power to
tread on snakes and scorpions and all the forces
of the enemy, and nothing shall ever injure you.'
(Lk. 10:18-19)..

One of the greatest teachings on the kingdom of God is
the Lord's Prayer *(See Matt.* 6:9-13 and *Lk.* 11:1-4). In this prayer, Jesus
taught His disciples to pray to the Father for the coming of

His kingdom. This is the heart of His prayer—*Father, Your kingdom come!* This prayer asks that the reign of Jesus be established among us, to the destruction of the kingdom of the evil one. When Jesus reigns in our hearts, then His kingdom is among us; He is among us, and we are delivered from the evil one. In this establishment of the kingdom of God, the Father is hallowed; His will is done on earth as it is in Heaven. His kingdom is established under the condition of our trust in His daily providential care and our forgiving, as we have been forgiven. This kingdom of God, already established in Heaven, is yet to be established on earth and this is why we pray, *Your kingdom come.*

When accused of casting out the devil by Beelzebub, the prince of devils, Jesus replied: *If it is by the finger of God* (read power of God) *that I cast out devils, then the reign of God is upon you.* (*Lk.* 11:20). When instructing His disciples about trust in God's providence in regard to our human needs He said: *Your Father knows that you need such things. Seek instead his kingship over you, and the rest will follow in turn. Do not live in fear, little flock. It has pleased your Father to give you the kingdom.* (*Lk.* 12:31-32).

Jesus also describes His role in establishing the kingdom of His Father in His prediction of His passion, death and resurrection (*See Lk.* 9:22, 44; 18:31-33). He speaks of this event as a fire and a baptism that will bring division.

He speaks of the signs of the inauguration of His kingdom and of His coming in glory (*See Lk.* 21: 5-36): *Likewise when you see all things happening of which I speak, know that the reign of God is near.*

At the supper, the night before He died, Jesus said to His apostles: *I have greatly desired to eat this Passover with you before I suffer. I tell you I will not eat again until it is fulfilled in the kingdom of God.* (*Lk.* 22:15-16). Then after celebrating the Eucharist with them, He gives them the dominion of the kingdom: *I for my part assign to you the dominion my Father has assigned to me. In my kingdom you will eat and drink at my table, and you will sit on thrones judging the twelve tribes of Israel.* (*Lk.* 22:24-30). Then follows those dreadful words of Jesus about Satan's desires: *Simon, Simon! Remember that Satan has asked for you* (all) *to sift you* (all) *like wheat. But I have prayed for you* (Peter) *that your faith may never fail. You* (Peter) *in turn must strengthen your brothers.* (*Lk.* 22:31-32).

After the supper, Jesus enters into battle with Satan. In the Garden of Olives, He sought the support of His disciples in the words reflecting the Lord's prayer: *Pray that you may not be put to the test* and then praying on His knees, *Father ...not my will but yours be done,* and just as with the temptation in the desert, an angel came from Heaven to strengthen Him. (*See Lk.* 22: 39-46). To the band of men led by Judas, whom Satan had entered, He said: *This is your hour—the triumph of darkness!* (*Lk.* 22:53).

And as the final irony, the King of the Father's kingdom, hanging on the cross, is correctly titled with the inscription over His head: "This is the King of the Jews!"

Just as St. Luke gives us a full picture of the spiritual war for the kingdom, so St. John provides clear insight on the Cross, as the victory over Satan, and acknowledges Satan as the "prince" of this world through these words of Our Lord.

> *Now has judgment come upon this world, now will this world's prince be driven out, and I—once I am lifted up from the earth—will draw all men to myself.* (*Jn.* 12:31-32).
> And again:
> *...the Prince of this world is at hand. He has no hold on me...* (*Jn.* 14:30).

In his letters, John makes clear the reason for the coming of Jesus Christ: *The man who sins belongs to the devil, because the devil is a sinner from the beginning. It was to destroy the devil's works that the Son of God revealed himself.* (*Jn.* 3:8). And he adds:
We know that we belong to God, while the whole world is under the evil one. (*Jn.* 5:19).

The spiritual warfare between the kingdom of God and the kingdom of darkness is described in a mystical way in the Book of Revelations. In Heaven, this battle is won and completed as described in Chapters four and five. But on earth, the battle now must be completed. *Revelations* 12 describes Satan's attacks on the offspring of the woman, who, on earth keeps the Lord's commandments and gives witness to Jesus. Then in Chapter 13, a parody of Christ and His prophets is presented. Satan (dragon) creates a beast which mocks the Resurrection. *In wonderment the whole world followed after the beast. Men worshiped the dragon for giving authority to the beast; they also worshiped the beast and said, 'Who can compare with the beast or come forward to fight against it.'* (Rev. 13:3-4).

In our generation we can see Satan using atheistic communism and atheistic consumerism to capture most of the nations and societies of the world. What nation and society has not succumbed to the lure of these forms of secularism?

But the parody goes on—a second beast, who was a spokesman and prophet of the first beast, is described: *It used the authority of the first beast to promote its interests by making the world and all its inhabitants worship the first beast, whose mortal wound had been healed. It performed great prodigies, it even made fire come down from heaven to earth, as men looked on.* (Rev. 13:11-13).

We can also see and hear Satan using the mass media to promote his interest. We can see and hear secularism in the hedonism, materialism, pornography, violence, and all forms of sin glorified in rock music, movies, TV, magazines, newspaper and radio broadcast and published around the world. What nation and what society has not been affected?

My personal experience in traveling in four continents, giving retreats to priests, has made me more aware of the work of Satan attacking the nations, societies and the Church with secularism. The attack of secularism must be identified and battled with the weapons of the Gospel of Jesus Christ.

A practical example of the attack of Satan by secularization is Ireland. Recently, a team of four priests from the Franciscan University of Steubenville were in Ireland speaking to groups of priests in Cork, Dublin and Belfast. We spoke to them about the need of forming support groups among priests, because of the nature and urgency of the times. They spoke to us of the devastating effect of secularism. A survey of the youth in Cork showed that 80% of the young considered the Church irrelevant, but fortunately, still saw Jesus Christ as relevant. Church attendance of youth and young adults (up to 30 years of age) is dramatically down throughout Ireland. Vocations to the priesthood and religious life are very low. Importing TV from the United States had made "Dallas" and "Dynasty" the two most popular shows! Dublin became a drug capital of Europe. Overall, the young are lost to the Church—due to a secular materialism that has swept the country. We shared with the priests our observation, and they concurred—"What penal persecutions couldn't do in four hundred years, secularism has done in ten years!"

What has happened to the Church in Holland in the past three decades is also an example of Satan's attack by secularism. A secular-theology and an independent liberalization has devastated vocations, emptied seminaries and churches. Progressively, a secular mindset took over the Catholic newspapers, the seminary faculties and the parish councils. A rift grew between the laity and hierarchy. Cardinal Johannes Willebrandis was asked by a group of American bishops while on a visit to the United States, "Where did the trouble begin? Holland was a leader in the Church and in missions around the world." The Cardinal answered, "The people became enamored with the concept of the priesthood of their baptism to the neglect of the órdained priesthood—it is a question of balance."

Consider the satanic effect secularism could have on societies. If the Soviet Union allowed an American lifestyle—with its principles, rock music and mass media, it would destroy itself. If the Soviet Union wanted to destroy the Church in Poland, the fastest way would be materialistic secularism. So far, their persecution of Poland has only strengthened the nation. The Church of Poland has repeatedly consecrated the nation to the Immaculate Heart of Mary and proclaimed her

Queen. The Church in Poland is vibrant, the churches are jammed, the seminaries are packed and the faith is strong. What has happened in the Church of Poland is a sign of hope for us in the battle against the satanic attack of secularism. The current threat to the Polish Church is, in fact, a growing secularism among the youth! Mary, protect them!

Truly, with St. Paul, we can say: *Our battle is not against human forces but against the principalities and powers, the rulers of this world of darkness, the evil spirits in regions above.* (*Eph.* 6:12).

CHAPTER 2

MARY'S ROLE IN SPIRITUAL WARFARE

O Mary, conceived without sin, pray for us who
have recourse to you.

Mary plays a key role in spiritual warfare. If we are able
to grasp the significance of her role in crushing Satan, then
we can better grasp the grandeur of God's plan.

Mary's role goes back to the rebellion of Lucifer (Satan).
When God created Lucifer (the "morning star" or "light
bearer") He created a magnificent being who shared in His
own freedom and power. And God respected His creature
and would not violate the freedom and power He gave Lucifer and the angels, even if they might abuse that power and
freedom. When Lucifer and his angels did in fact rebel with
a cry, "I will not serve," it was over the issue of the Son
of God becoming incarnate—born of a woman by the power
of the Holy Spirit. God revealed His plan, that He would
save man from sin by lowering Himself below the angels by
becoming man. In doing so, Lucifer would thus be lower than
the woman and her offspring. Such a humiliation was just
too much for Lucifer and his angels and they rebelled. The
words of Isaiah can be applied to this rebellion:

*How have you fallen from the heavens, O morn-
ing star (Lucifer), son of the dawn! How are you
cut down to the ground, you who moved the
nations! You said in your heart: 'I will scale the
heavens; Above the stars of God I will set up my
throne; I will take my seat on the Mount of Assembly, in the recesses of the north. I will ascend above*

the tops of the clouds; I will be like the Most High!'
Yet down to the nether world you go to the recesses
of the pit! (*Is.* 14:12-15).

This magnificent creature of God, the light bearer, the morning star, along with his angels sinned against God with a rebellious cry of pride, "I will not serve!"
The Book of Revelation describes the war in which rebellious Lucifer (now called Satan) was cast out of the heavens:

> *Then war broke out in heaven: Michael and his angels battled against the dragon. Although the dragon and his angels fought back, they were overpowered and lost their place in heaven. The huge dragon, the ancient serpent known as the devil or Satan, the seducer of the whole world, was driven out; he was hurled down to earth and his minions with him.* (*Rev.* 12:7-9).

Satan's continued rage has been directed against the woman who gave birth to the Saviour and against the members of His body, also her offspring, the Church:

> *Enraged at her escape, the dragon went off to make war on the rest of her offspring, on those who keep God's commandments and give witness to Jesus.* (*Rev.* 12:17).

God's answer to the rebellious Lucifer is Mary. Mary is God's perfect creation, the new morning star replacing Lucifer. She is the "Ark of the Covenant" (*Rev.* 11:19) bearing the Lord of the New Covenant. She is the great sign which appeared in the sky, *a woman clothed with the sun, with the moon under her feet, and on her head a crown of twelve stars* (*Rev.* 12:1). Mary is God's perfect creation who was immaculately conceived, and so was never under the domain of Satan or of sin.

Mary's response to the angel of the Lord, *I am the servant of the Lord. Let it be done to me as you say* (*Lk.* 1:38), is the perfect rebuttal to Lucifer's, "I will not serve!" Mary's canticle, in response to Elizabeth's greeting, is the perfect response to Lucifer's pride:

My being proclaims the greatness of the Lord,
my spirit finds joy in God my Saviour. For he has
looked upon his servant in her lowliness; all ages
to come shall call me blessed. God who is mighty
has done great things for me, holy is his name;
his mercy is from age to age on those who fear
him. He has shown might with his arm; he has con-
fused the proud in their inmost thoughts. He has
deposed the mighty from their thrones and has
raised the lowly to high places. The hungry he has
given every good thing, while the rich he has sent
empty away. He has upheld Israel his servant, ever
mindful of his mercy; even as he promised our
fathers, promised Abraham and his descendents
forever. (*Lk.* 1:46-55).

Mary's response of praise, of humility, of service, and of
mercy is in direct opposition to Satan's self-gratification of
rebellion, pride, unwillingness to serve, hatred and accusa-
tion. Mary, the servant of the Lord, gives birth to the suffering Servant, who by his obedience, humility, docility and love
defeats Satan on the cross.

Mary cooperated in the passion with her compassion, as
she stood at the cross of Jesus, and her heart too was pierced
with the sword of sorrow (*See Lk.* 2:35). By her cooperation,
Mary's continued and renewed "yes" of the Annunciation
became the "yes" that crushes the head of Satan.

Mary's Son and His body, the Church, continue to crush
the head of Satan. In Mary's Offspring is fulfilled the prophetic
word:

I will put enmity between you and the woman,
and between your offspring and hers; he will strike
at your head, while you strike at his heel. (*Gen.* 3:15).

The Second Vatican Council developed the grandeur of
Mary's role in two passages that speak of her Immaculate
Conception:

It is no wonder, then, that the usage prevailed
among the holy Fathers whereby they called the

*Mother of God entirely holy and free from all stain
of sin, fashioned by the Holy Spirit into a new kind
of substance and new creature. Adorned from the
first instant of her conception with the splendors
of an entirely unique holiness, the Virgin of Nazareth
is, on God's command, greeted by an angel messenger as "full of grace." To the heavenly messenger
she replies: "Behold the handmaid of the Lord: be
it done to me according to thy word.*

(*Lumen Gentium*, #57) (*See Reference 3*).

In the second passage, Mary's Queenship is described. She
shares in the victory of her Son, the Lord of lords:

*Finally, preserved free from all guilt of original
sin, the Immaculate Virgin was taken up body and
soul into heavenly glory upon completion of her
earthly sojourn. She was exalted by the Lord as
Queen of All, in order that she might be the more
thoroughly conformed to her Son, the Lord of lords
and conqueror of sin and death.*

(*Lumen Gentium*, #59) (*See Reference 3*).

Mary is God's perfect answer and rebuttal to the rebellion
of Lucifer. Mary is also the instrument chosen by God to
crush Satan. It is her flesh—the Word made flesh, and His
body, the Church, that crushes Satan. It is the flesh and blood
of Jesus, born of Mary by the power of the Holy Spirit, present among us in the Eucharist, that makes present that victory.

The uniqueness of Mary's role in spiritual warfare is that
it is God's plan. The Lord God chose a human being, a
woman, someone totally human, to be the instrument of His
victory over Satan and his followers. The Lord chose the way
of humility and mercy to defeat pride and rebellion. And
Jesus, the Son of the Father and Son of Mary carried out
this plan:

*What is man that you should be mindful of him,
or the son of man that you should care for him?
You made him little less than the angels and crowned
him with glory and honor. You have given him rule*

over the works of your hands, putting all things under his feet. (Ps. 8:5-7).

Mary is God's choice. God uniquely chose Mary to be the Immaculate mother of His only Son. She and no other was chosen by God for this role. Who are we to disagree.

> *For all the saving influences of the Blessed Virgin on men originate, not from some inner necessity, but from the divine pleasure. They flow from the superabundance of the merits of Christ, rest on His mediation, depend entirely on it, and draw all their power from it. In no way do they impede the immediate union of the faithful with Christ. Rather, they foster this union.*
>
> (*Lumen Gentium* #60) *(See Reference 3).*

The issue is **sin**. Satan sinned and is the father of sin. He tempted Adam and Eve to sin and he continues to tempt us to sin. God's plan for victory over Satan was to take on our sin: *For our sakes God made him* (Jesus) *who did not know sin to be sin, so that in him we might become the very holiness of God.* (2 Cor. 5:21).

In God's plan for victory, Mary was the first to share in this holiness, this sinlessness, through her Immaculate Conception. Because she is sinless, Satan has no hold on her as he has no hold on Jesus. Because she is sinless, God's power flows through her without any hindrance. Because she is sinless, she is God's answer to the father of sin. Because she is sinless, God has chosen to use her to defeat Satan in his attacks on us.

Mary's part in the plan to defeat Satan's hold on us, which he has through sin, is to share with us her sinlessness. She wants to make us immaculate—a glorious bride of Christ, "holy and immaculate, without stain or wrinkle or anything of that sort." (Eph. 5:27). Her plan is to clothe us in her own holiness. She wants us free from sin, the only thing that keeps us in the kingdom of Satan.

Mary has been teaching us how to be free of sin. Her message at Lourdes is that she is the Immaculate Conception—totally free of sin. Then her message at Fatima teaches us how to share in that grace—by repentance from sin, by doing reparation for sin, and by consecration to her Immaculate Heart which is a refuge from sin and an immersion in her holiness. Her message was that her Immaculate Heart would finally triumph. Today, she is echoing these same messages all over the world.

The issue of spiritual warfare is certainly sin—our personal sin, our corporate sin, and the sin of rebellion of Satan and all who follow him. The victory over sin is the Cross of Jesus, where, by His passion and death, He claims the victory of resurrection over sin, death and Satan. Mary's role is to bring us to that perfect sinlessness, that immaculateness which is hers through the victory of her Son. Mary already is, what all of us are called to be—immaculate.

Our Part in Mary's Role

Our part in Mary's role flows from the dual commission which Jesus gave on the cross—to Mary and to us, His disciples. Jesus extended Mary's motherhood to include us, and then He gave us His own mother, that we might be children of the Mother of God! *(See Pope John Paul II's homily at Fatima, May 13, 1982 in the Appendix)*.

In this secularized age, we especially need to share in these virtues of Mary that stand in direct contrast and contradiction to Satan. We want to share in her purity and humility. Her purity is a total transparent immaculateness of body, mind, and heart. Her humility is true, docile, simple and silent. These weapons of purity and humility will defeat the tactics of Satan. He uses sex and rebellion to infect us with secularism. This secularism is the disease of our times and the antidote to this infection of Satan is the total "yes" of Mary to the Lord, a "yes" that is simple, single, and strong. It is a "yes" we need to give.

All of Mary's graces are graces that are shared with us. She received them in perfection—as a model of what is in store for us:

In the most holy Virgin, the Church has already reached that perfection whereby she exists without

*spot or wrinkle. . . Seeking after the glory of Christ,
the Church becomes more like her exalted model,
and continually progresses in faith, hope and char-
ity, searching out and doing the will of God in all
things.* (*Lumen Gentium,* #65) (See Reference 3).

As members of the Church, we share in Mary's Immaculate Conception, her motherhood, her redemptive compassion and her grace of Assumption and Queenship. We too
are to reign with Christ, as His Bride. This means that we
too are to share in the spiritual warfare and the victory. We
are the body of Christ and we are the children of Mary.

How do we become the "humble servants of the Lord?"
We become the humble servants of the Lord by submitting
ourselves to the tutelage of Mary. She will teach us and bring
us to her sinlessness, her holiness and will prepare us for
the victorious battle of the Cross—even as she prepared Jesus!
She will bring us to His docility to the will of the Father,
to His humility, to His obedience, to His forgiveness and to
His love which transformed suffering into salvation. We need
to enroll ourselves in her school of holiness by entrusting
our lives to her by consecration. By consecration, we allow
Mary to fulfill the Lord's plans both for her and for us.

So in a practical way, each day we can enter into Mary's
role of crushing the head of Satan by renewing the consecration of our lives to her. Here are two acts of Consecration
to Mary that invite her to do for us, what she did for Jesus.

Act of Consecration
to the Immaculate Heart of Mary
(St. Louis de Montfort's Consecration)

"I.N., a faithless sinner—renew and ratify today
in your hands, O Immaculate Mother, the vows of
my Baptism; I renounce forever Satan, his pomps
and works; and I give myself entirely to Jesus Christ,
the Incarnate Wisdom, to carry my cross after Him
all the days of my life, and to be more faithful to
Him than I have ever been before.

"In the presence of all the heavenly court I choose

you this day for my Mother and Queen. I deliver and consecrate to you, as your slave, my body and soul, my goods, both interior and exterior, and even the value of all my good actions, past, present and future; leaving to you the entire and full right of disposing of me, and all that belongs to me, without exception, according to your good pleasure, for the greater glory of God, in time and in eternity. Amen."

Act of Consecration
To Mary

Mary, Mother of Jesus and Mother of Mercy, since Jesus from the Cross gave you to me, I take you as my own. And since Jesus gave me to you, take me as your own. Make me docile like Jesus on the Cross, obedient to the Father, trusting in humility and in love.

Mary, my Mother, in imitation of the Father, Who gave His Son to you, I too give my all to you; to you I entrust all that I am, all that I have and all that I do. Help me to surrender ever more fully to the Spirit. Lead me deeper into the Mystery of the Cross, the Cenacle and the fullness of Church. As you formed the heart of Jesus by the Spirit, form my heart to be the throne of Jesus in His glorious coming. *(See Reference 15)*.

We can also pray that the graces and victory Mary enjoys may be ours as well. In response to the teaching of the fathers of the Second Vatican Council, we pray:

Mary, Our Mother

Mary, our mother, Queen of Heaven, all generations call you blessed, for in you the kingdom has come! You have fulfilled the Father's will. Prepare our hearts on earth, for the reign of Jesus; care for us; feed us; crush the head of the evil one. Amen.

O Mary, conceived without sin, pray for us who have recourse to you. *(See Reference 16)*.

CHAPTER 3

A SPECIAL POINT OF ATTACK: PRIESTS!

Satan has attacked priests, and the priesthood of the Church, like no other group, knowing that in this way he is attacking the source of power in the Church. Priests make present the sacrificial Body and Blood of Jesus on altars around the world, and as long as priests are holy and continue their priestly worship, Satan and his forces are bound. So the most concentrated attack of Satan has been on priests. We can see this in their low morale, their decreased numbers and their harrassment.

Priests need special love, prayer and support! The whole Church needs to be made aware of this, especially bishops and priests themselves. Priests, and those in charge of the spiritual welfare of priests, need to be aware of this concentrated attack and construct a concentrated defense through faith and prayer, the armor of God.

My observations of the state of the priesthood come from contact with over 2,000 priests at Bethany House of Intercession. Over an eight year period, we carried on a daily program of intercessory prayer for the bishops, priests and deacons of the Church. Joining our core group of five or six, priests came from all over the world, some 1,400 for one day to a month's stay to pray for brother priests. Other contacts were made with priests and religious at dozens of retreats and conferences. Through sharing our lives and prayer, I have come to form some definite impressions on the state of the priesthood.

What I am concerned about comes mainly from my contact with priests in the last decade, but I see the same situa tions in the life of religious, and in the Church overall.

I am concerned about the extent of secularization that has infiltrated our lives. A pattern of thinking, values, behavior, attitudes, methodologies, and priorities has so influenced us that, at times, it is difficult to distinguish between world values and Gospel values. In a sense, the world has evangelized the Church faster than the Church has evangelized the world!

Eternity, eternal life, and the last things—death, judgment, Hell and Heaven, have been re-evaluated and re-interpreted in a secular, here and now, down to earth way, so that the sense of the transcendence and mystery of God has virtually evaporated.

What are the results of this? Look around to religious houses, rectories, seminaries. We can all too easily find examples of affluence, the best in food, in clothes, in entertainment, in travel, in vacations, in the lastest electronic gadgetry, borderline moral behavior, confused sexual relationships, libraries containing books that do not build up faith or are the direct cause of temptation and sin. And worse yet, we find a lot of confused priests and religious, who are in turmoil, isolated, mentally and emotionally drained with no apparent way to reach out to them with compassion, forgiveness, healing and spiritual freedom.

To put it in one word, the state of priests and religious is weak. There is confusion, a lack of discipline, a failure to hold fast to the fundamentals of the Gospel. There is too much darkness and depression, nurtured by growing disobedience and infatuation with "new age" concepts.

All of the priests who came to pray with us at Bethany House of Intercession were given an opportunity to express their priestly needs so that the community might intercede for them. By far, a very major problem expressed over and over again was "isolation." Priests and religious are isolated. Isolated from each other, not only geographically at times, but more significantly, spiritually and emotionally. There is real isolation and loneliness. Sometimes the greatest isolation is in a rectory or religious house with others present under the same roof, but without real communication, conversation, sharing, or friendship. It all usually surfaces with dissatisfaction with the Church.

There is a general "confusion" about the truth. What is the truth of Sacred Scripture? What is the truth taught by the Church? Such questions are common, because they have been planted in our minds by scholars who have been questioning and searching without a basic foundation of faith, without a Christian community that is living out its faith in a daily way.

Our minds, already darkened by original sin, are even more confused by philosophical systems that deny the possibility of knowing the truth, so that all knowledge becomes subjective. The very possibility, and ability, to know God in a personal way is denied, or at least obscured.

Lifting of some restraints of discipline, as a result of the Second Vatican Council, has opened the floodgates for many. The discipline of Christian life has evaporated, and the daily lifestyle has reflected this in the schedule of prayer, work, rest and recreation. I would venture to say that most of us have been influenced by the lifting of restraints as seen by our own schedules, our reading habits, our recreations, and our associations. It would be interesting to examine and compare the "before and after" of the Council in terms of our ascetical practices. What has happened to penance? To mortification? To fasting? To prayer? To vigils? To dedication to our household tasks of service?

Has our **faith** in Jesus Christ as Lord and Redeemer become deeper? More personal? More trusting? More committed? More faithful? Each of us needs to examine our own hearts in this matter. But it seems that the criteria for judging our faith has become the extent of our social involvement with "great causes" rather than a greater union with Christ Jesus as the source of our life and power.

Faith in Jesus Christ places us in the kingdom of God and places us in conflict with the kingdom of the world. Without faith, we cannot please God; we can only please mankind. Faith in Jesus Christ is the key issue. Is He really the center and focus of all that we are and all that we do?

Some priests and religious appear to be in a malaise. A state of lethargy says, "I've had it. I've tried all these various programs. They haven't worked. I don't want to try anything more. Just leave me alone. I'm tired out. I'm burned out. I don't want to get involved with anything."

This kind of malaise is seen in the lack of attendance at conferences, at special retreat days, at workshops. It is a complacency that is seen as a general non-response to the movement of God's graces. It is a lack of zeal that makes it impossible to take on an apostolic offensive. It expresses itself in busy-ness—more meetings, more committees.

"Busy-ness" is an escape. We've become so busy, and understandably so with the growing lack of personnel, that we do not have the time for the fundamentals. Busy-ness can be an escape from the real issues at hand, especially the time it takes daily to seek the face of the Lord and His plan for our lives each day. Busy-ness can be an escape from the pain in our lives—the hurts, the confusion, the isolation. Through busy-ness we can escape from ourselves and escape from God—but not for long. The "Hound of Heaven" is relentless. The response of the first apostles to busy-ness was to appoint seven deacons to take care of the temporal needs with the expressed reason that, *This will permit us to concentrate on prayer and the ministry of the Word.* (*Acts* 6:4).

This is a time of *God's special visitation.* It is a time of God showering His mercy upon us through His interventions in such graces as the Second Vatican Council, the recent popes, renewals, and apparitions of Mary. It is also a time of tribulation and testing as seen by the "lack of peace" *(Dives in Misericordia, John Paul II) (See Reference 5)* in our lives and in the unsettlement of nature. It is a time of God's judgment of mercy as He lifts His protective hand of mercy to reveal the horror of our sins. It is a time when God will shake us to come to the awareness of what we have done—the creation of a society without Him—turned to the worship of creatures rather than the worship of the Creator. (*See Romans* 1:18-32).

This visitation is a sovereign action of God. He is intervening in our lives to bring us back to Him. God is acting sovereignly in calling us to return to Him. The Lord is preparing us for His coming. God is acting in a sovereign way so that Jesus Christ might be the center and focus of our lives, that He might be all in all.

The hope for renewal of the priesthood and religious life lies only in Jesus Christ. Without a renewal of our relationship with Him, we are not renewing ourselves or the Church. Renewal will only come with a renewal of our hearts and minds by a new and deeper conversion to Jesus Christ. There is no new program, no new technique, no new workshop or new organizational device that will renew the priesthood or religious life.

The way things are going, many priests and religious may not hear this radical call to conversion. Perhaps only a remnant will hear and act upon it. This kind of hope in a remnant may seem pessimistic, but I rather see it as realistic in this secularized world.

Our hope of renewal is based on the coming of the Lord Jesus. The fact that He is coming again is our faith. We will be renewed when we live with the daily expectancy of His coming—ready and vigilant, waiting in prayer, ready to greet Him. We will be renewed when we live prepared to welcome Him as though He were to come again in this twenty-four hours. It is this kind of urgency and expectancy that typifies a renewed Church. To live in a self-satisfied, rationalizing way is to live in ignorant bliss, unaware of God's plan for renewal.

What can we do to prepare for His coming? The best way to prepare for the coming of our Lord Jesus Christ is to live fully as Christians—to live fully a life of faith and repentance in the kingdom. This is the basic gospel message Jesus preached: *This is the time of fulfillment. The reign of God is at hand! Reform your lives and believe in the Gospel!* (Mk. 1:15). This is the same message currently being delivered by the mother of Christ in many places of our world today.

The faith that gives me hope is faith in Jesus Christ Our Saviour and Our Lord. A deep faith in Christ Jesus, Son of God and Son of Mary, that is based not on feelings or passing emotional highs, but on a **commitment** to be faithful to Him—at all times, in dark times as well as in times of light. I see this faith lived out in the daily lives of a growing number of lay people who are members of covenant communities. They live a lifestyle based on faith in Jesus Christ as seen in the fruit of their lives, namely, a life of repentance, prayer, service and peaceful order. They live in the kingdom of God.

These Christian lay communities are a great sign of hope for the Church, and priests and religious need to look to the faith of these people, because much can be learned by examining their way of life. It is not an easy task to keep our hearts and minds turned away from this secularized world around us, and to turn again and again to the Lord. Everything around us calls us to self and self-exaltation. In the midst of this, to see whole families joyfully living a life of repentance from self, self-concern and sin is cause for great hope.

It is a sign of hope too, to see men and women in communities and prayer groups being formed to be servants, and to honor the role of the servant. To have the heart of a servant is a special gift and goal. It is to have the heart of Jesus Himself, Who came to serve, not to be served. In Christian covenanted communities, prayer and fasting is a normal part of Christian life. Each day, the members seek the face of the Lord in prayer and gather together in assembly to worship the Lord. They reinforce their prayer with fasting. Some fast on bread and water alone once a week. There is also a "system of love," where everyone in the community or group is cared for. Each person is in a small group in which they are cared for by a pastoral leader who takes concern for their lives. The leader, in turn, is in a pastoral care group of leaders so that no one is left isolated and alone. This kind of pastoral care is not easy, because it involves submission, humility, and an ordered life. But this kind of pastoral care makes living the gospel possible in our times. This is real hope. We priests and religious need to rediscover a system of pastoral care.

But a warning is needed here. This system of pastoral care

is not a matter of group dynamics or psychological techniques. It is rather a question of formation under spiritual headship. The spiritual leader is like a gardener who knows how to prepare the soil and foster the growth of the plant to bring forth fruit. This kind of formation demands a teaching that *forms* the person in a way of living; it doesn't just inform or inspire. There is need of special teachings and special teachers.

The covenant communities have developed teachings that form men and women with the wisdom of the Sacred Scripture. Life in the Spirit Seminars lead people to deeper conversion to Christ and a full release of the Holy Spirit. Courses on the foundations of Christian living deal with such things as sin and wrong-doing in our lives, emotions, authority, married and single life, living the fruit of the Spirit, living in community, prayer, Christian discipline and order in our lives, deliverance from evil spirits and growth in holiness.

It is this kind of formational teaching that needs to be introduced into our formation programs. We need not only information and inspiration, we need formation as well. We need to be taught the very practical "how to's" of living in the kingdom.

Other signs of hope I have seen are a renewed awareness and devotion to Mary, a rediscovery of the power of intercession for God's mercy, and also, a new society of priests. Mary's role in the Divine plan for our salvation is being rediscovered. There is a new awareness that God has chosen Mary to cooperate in the Incarnation and Redemption of Jesus Christ. There is a new awareness among the communities of her special role as our Mother as well as our model. There is growing knowledge and freedom in speaking and teaching about her role and her apparitions. There is a greater devotion growing with regular prayer of the rosary, and renewed consecration to Mary.

Interceding for the needs of the Church and world has become part of the daily life of many communities. It is a common practice to set aside regular times to gather together in order to intercede before the Blessed Sacrament. The awareness of our role as intercessors has awakened a renewed cry of "Lord have mercy on us and on the whole world." It is only God's sovereign action of pouring out His mercy that is the source of our hope. There is a new intensity in the cry, "Come, Lord Jesus! Come, Lord Jesus and renew Your Church, renew the face of the earth."

What hope do I see for the third millenium? I hope for a "third day" experience. *In the Lord's eyes, one day is as a thousand years and a thousand years are as a day.* (2 Ptr. 3:8). This coming third thousand may well be the "new advent" written about by Pope John Paul II, in *Redemptor Hominis. (See Reference 6).* It well may be the "third day," the day of resurrection. May our preparation for the coming of the Lord by renewal and re-formation into mature Christians hasten the Day of the Lord.

What practical steps can be taken to renew a religious community? Over the past fifteen years of working with the renewal of priests, I've experienced some things that bore fruit to a certain degree and other attempts that were not so successful. I would like to suggest three things that have produced fruit and could be used in renewal of a religious community:

1. Retreats leading to the baptism in the Holy Spirit,
2. Community intercession, and,
3. Fraternity groups among priests.

In conducting over one hundred retreats for priests that prepared for the experience of baptism in the Holy Spirit, I came to see, repeatedly, priests' lives changed and a new power released in their lives. Baptism in the Holy Spirit is clearly based on Sacred Scripture and has been clearly explained theologically in a number of ways, and encouraged by various episcopal conferences and two popes (Paul VI and John Paul II). The baptism in the Holy Spirit should be made available to all. We should not allow prejudice toward the Charismatic or Pentecostal movement, to prevent us from experiencing what is promised us in the Gospel. What the Charismatic Renewal has shown us is that the baptism in the Holy Spirit can be prepared for and received by prayer and laying on of hands. This kind of retreat can be made available to all.

Over an eight year period, a core group of four to six of us, joined by visiting priests (some 2,000 of them), carried on a daily program of intercession for bishops, priests, and deacons of the Church. It was a work of faith and only God can judge the effect of the prayers over the years. But judging by the effect on us in the core (12 of us over the eight years), and the effect on those who joined in our intercession, we saw new life and healing flowing into the men. A serious program of intercession is something that can be done and should be done as a step toward renewal of communities.

There are various types of fraternity groups among priests that offer support. However, because of the strong attack against priests, a special type of group is needed to support them in the battle. Since 1983, a team of priests working out of the Franciscan University of Steubenville, (Ohio) has been promoting and setting up local fraternities of priests to respond to the current need. The local fraternity is a group of priests committed to meeting weekly to worship God in praise, to receive formational teaching, and to receive pastoral care in small groups. What has been learned from the covenanted lay communities is adapted to priests' fraternity groups.

We feel that this kind of strong commitment to the Lord and to one another is needed to respond to the urgency of the times. It gives us hope that strong and renewed priests will be a significant force in the renewal of the Church. Although all priests are not ready for this kind of commitment, we rejoice with those who have made the commitment and are growing in strength.

CHAPTER 4

SATAN'S BATTLE AGAINST THE WOMAN

Today, we are living out the twelfth chapter of the Book of Revelation, and the battle is on. But the victory has been promised to the woman (*See Gen.* 3:15); Satan and his minions have been thrown out of Heaven. (*See Rev.* 12:7-8). Now the battle is on earth (*See Rev.* 12:9), and what has already happened in Heaven is now to happen on earth. The battle encompasses the whole Bible, from the first Book of Genesis to the final Book of Revelation.

Today, the battle is especially painful because there is precise aggression against women, against all sexual identity and unique roles, and against the unique maternal role of THE woman as "mother of the living." The battle against the woman has confused and angered this generation of women, and men as well. The confusion is such that we are fighting each other and do not recognize the enemy, nor do most even know of his existence. Satan has so confused our minds over the centuries that now he can freely attack the fundamental identity of both men and women without being identified as the enemy!

The battle has become so obscured that we cannot even dialogue about it. Our vocabulary is confused by changes in the use of standard words; our language and categories of grammar are destroyed, along with our mutual trust. Competition, anger, rebellious independence is more the style of communication than compassion, understanding, encouragement, mutual assistance and cooperation. Even in writing this, I have little hope that a "liberated woman" would be able to accept it, or want to read it. Nevertheless, this message of Satan's battle against woman needs to be made clear. Satan has attacked the woman, all sexual roles, sexuality, and life itself.

The consequences of this attack of Satan are seen in the changed morality in regard to the purpose of the sexual union, birth control, abortion, adultery, divorce and family life, euthanasia, biological manipulation of the genes *in vitro*, the rebellious attitude of some women in the secular woman's liberation movements, the explosion of pornography and violence in the media, and a general disregard for life in the build up of nuclear arms and growing political injustices. This is such a mammoth list that we need to examine it for a "root cause," to better see the pattern, and the point of Satan's attack.

In the *"Ratzinger Report,"* *(See Reference 7)* Cardinal Ratzinger gives an insight into the point of attack, namely, the fatal rupture between sexuality and procreation. He explains that sexual specificity has been trivialized, making every role interchangeable between men and women, and an artificial distinction has been made between sex and life. Sex has become a matter of pleasure; life has become something we control for our convenience. We want to be free of the "Slavery of nature."

This is the same basic attack (against all mankind), that Satan waged against Adam and Eve: *You will be like gods...* *(Gen. 3:5).* We, too, are continually tempted to be like God in our own way, through our control and our so-called liberation from the "Slavery of nature." We have suddenly discovered new age freedoms—they were first promised by Satan.

Pope Paul VI in "Humanae Vitae" (1968) *(See Reference 8)* prophetically wrote of this kind of attack against sexuality and life. His letter is more an expressive concern for the Church's teaching authority on the natural law, than a regulation of birth. In re-reading the encyclical sympathetically, I could feel his compassion, his agony, and tears for the Church and for married couples. In the section on the consequences of methods of artificial birth control, he described in prophetic words the open road to infidelity, to lowering of morality and of respect for women, and ultimate government control of the family. Since then, we in the United States alone have seen the predicted consequences explode around us: pornography, fifteen million abortions in a decade, sterilization, negative and positive euthanasia, "test tube" babies, gay rights, women's radical liberalization movements, and a skyrocketing divorce rate. There need not be a direct causative relationship in these events, but once the door is opened to a contraceptive mentality, there is no limit to man's arbitrary control of body and functions.

Satan seems to have used this encyclical to drive a wedge between the teaching authority of the Church and many scholars in the Church. Supreme Court judges of the United States quickly sensed a crack in the strong position of the American bishops on marriage morality after the publication of "Humanae Vitae," and so the court could pass their verdict legalizing abortions and allowing pornography! Their judgment was correct, because there was a minimal outcry from the Church at the time. I think we, as Catholics, have a lot of reparation to do for not supporting the prophetic stance of Pope Paul VI on birth control with greater zeal! We now see the consequences of Satan's attack.

We Are In Spiritual Warfare

Because we are in spiritual warfare, we need to be aware of this terrible reality and act accordingly.

The fundamental reality, however, is that Jesus Christ has already gained the victory on the Cross. The victory is secured in Heaven; now it must be carried out on earth, and it has been given over to the Woman, to Mary Immaculate, Mother of God and our mother. Now, the decision must be made for or against her. It is a case of "either-or." There is no "in between," or "both-and." The victory is the Woman's or it is not! If it is the Woman's as prophesied in *Genesis* 3:15, pictured in *Revelation* 12, and emphasized by the messages of Our Lady at Fatima, then we had better get with her! She is telling us as much today.

Satan is attacking the Woman, the New Eve, the Mother of Jesus Christ, the Mother of God, the Mother of the Church. Satan is attacking her by attacking her offspring, especially those who are called to be like her and her Son:

> *Enraged at her escape, the dragon (Satan) went off to make war on the rest of her offspring, on those who keep God's commandments and give witness to Jesus.* (Rev. 12:17).

It is important in this warfare, that we fully understand that we have been duped by Satan into trying to be "like gods" rather than being God's. As someone pointed out, it's a matter of an apostrophe! We need to understand that we are to be like God, but in the way He had chosen for His Son Jesus Christ, and that is the way of obedience, of humility, of freedom according to our nature. When there is rebellion, disrespect for our nature, and pride, then we have succumbed to Satan.

Satan, the imposter and imitator, creates a beast who is worshiped in place of God (See Rev. 13:1-10) but was slain. He creates a second beast who resurrects the first—a parody of the Resurrection. He also creates a harlot, a parody of the Woman. (See Rev. 17). We have been duped into worshipping Satan's imitations.

The specific attack of Satan is against the Woman, Mary, because the victory is hers, and because she has been elevated above all the angels and saints by God's choice. She is now greater than what Lucifer used to be! This has so enraged Satan that he, in his final attack, has penetrated into the very nature of man and woman and into the nature of human life. Just one example from the list of consequences from Satan's attacks, given earlier, will serve to illustrate this.

Abortion: Some 1.5 million abortions a year have been performed in the United States alone, an estimated 15 million per year throughout the world. 150 million abortions this past decade! Aborted children who are not now with us on earth because of mankind's choice of control over nature. What a loss to this world! I thank God my mother didn't abort me. Thank God that Mary didn't have an abortion!

What terrible psychological damage has been done to the mothers of these unborn children, five, ten, twenty years later. What terrible spiritual damage has been done to their souls!

The Rebellious Attitude

One of the most potentially explosive issues of the Church in the United States is the role of women. The Bishops of the United States, under the committee chairmanship of Bishop Joseph Imesch of Joliet, IL. began to prepare a statement on the role of women. They conducted consultations with women in various dioceses in the country. The one I had contact with was a disaster, because of the secular method of gathering opinions. The question of the role of women was on the agenda of the extraordinary Synod of Bishops in Rome, November 24 to December 7, 1985. During the session, an American woman dressed as a priest, attempted to offer Mass at St. Peter's Basilica, until she was arrested. Speeches from women's liberation groups cried out: "How dare these men speak out for all of us?!"

Yes, there is deep hurt. Yes, there has been and is abuse in the Church. But the resolution will not be found in following the methodologies used by non-Christian, secular organizations. If there is no mercy, no repentance, no forgiveness, then there is no Christianity. Satan has used this period of women's roles and women's rights to twist the Church around into potential apostasy. Bishops and others who refuse to support Catholic Doctrine hasten its coming.

Let me give a specific picture of the tension over proposed ordination of women among some of the religious. I made an appointment with a Sister, the Superior General of a community, to discuss with her the relationships of priests and sisters. I knew Sister well and respected her judgment, so I freely spoke of the problem that many priests have brought to me. "How are priests to relate these days to the religious women that want to be ordained priests?"

I first told her my personal observation, that I see many angry women, with a cause, driven and acting with goals and dynamics that are identical with those of secular organizations. If the goals and methodologies are identical inside the Church with those outside the Church, then who has evangelized whom? I told Sister that our approach to the situation has been to intercede for the Lord's mercy. Sister's response confirmed my observations, and she went further. She said: "Things have come to a point where dialogue is impossible; it is beyond dialogue. At present these women are unable, not just unwilling, to hear any other point of view, especially coming from a male, above all a priest or bishop! The only recourse now is pleading God's mercy." She went on to say that she had to deal with two of her sisters that week who wanted to switch communities to one that would allow preparation for ordination to priesthood!

The battle is on. But how unfortunate that the real enemy is not identified and his goals and strategy not studied. We are like defenseless pawns!

The victory of Our Lord Jesus Christ has been given to the Woman, the Immaculate One, the Virgin Mary. If we truly are spiritual people, then we should see clearly with the eyes of faith what is happening and what needs to be done. We need to turn to the Woman, to Mary, and do what she requests of us. Over and over again, she calls us: "To do whatever He tells us!" namely, to keep His commandments and give witness to Jesus. She has pleaded with us to repent from sin, to pray and to sacrifice for sinners, and to entrust our consecrated lives to her that she may protect and care for us as mother. She needs us to be her children, like her Son Jesus, so that the victory given to her may be accomplished in us and in our day. That message comes with great urgency in her apparitions, multiplying in this century.

Mary, the Immaculate Conception, who like Jesus, is sinless and on whom Satan has no hold, wants to share her graces with us. We too, are to be sinless so Satan would have no hold on us. We too, are to share in her virginal spousal and maternal roles: virginal in that we are totally open only to God; spousal in that we are in a communion with the Lord our Bridegroom; maternal in that we are fruitful in bringing forth Jesus.

Today, we are living in times of spiritual warfare and in times of confusion and darkness. But we have our hope in the victory of Jesus Christ given to the Woman. When things are the darkest and seem to have totally collapsed, then we shall see resurrection and the victory! The final defeat of Satan and his minions will be the glory of the Lord and His angels and saints. What has already happened in Heaven is to be completed on earth.

CHAPTER 5
SPIRITUAL WARFARE

On November 15, 1972, during a General Audience, Pope Paul VI gave an address called "Deliver Us From Evil." His words revealed his concern about spiritual warfare:

> "What are the greatest needs of the Church today? Do not let our answer surprise you as being over-simple or even superstitious and unreal: One of the greatest needs is defense from that evil which is the Devil."

He goes on to describe the grandeur of God's creation and salvation, and then confronts the question of evil:

> "Evil is not merely a lack of something, but an effective agent, a living, spiritual being, perverted and perverting, a terrible reality. Mysterious and frightening. So we know that this dark and disturbing spirit really exists, and that he still acts with treacherous cunning. He is the secret enemy that sows errors and misfortunes in human history."

The Holy Father then challenges us to study this question:

> "This question of the Devil and the influence he can exert on individual persons as well as our communities, whole societies or events, is a very important chapter of Catholic doctrine which is given little attention today, though it should be studied again."

Origins of the Evil Spirits and Spiritual Warfare

The origins of evil spirits and spiritual warfare are symbolically described in Sacred Scripture, in the traditions of the Church, *(See Reference 9),* and through various saintly scholars and mystics who filled in the details of this significant, yet hidden event. The details vary, but the core of the picture is consistent: God created spirits to share in His freedom and power. He also created the visible world and man (both genders intended) within it, to share in His love and freedom. It would seem that the plan to create man with freedom would involve the possibility of mankind abusing that freedom by sinning, and here God's love and humility would be revealed. The Word would become man, born of a woman, and save all from their sins. This was at the center of the issue. God would humble Himself out of love to become a man, humble Himself below the angelic spirits that He created.

This humility was too much for one of the leaders of the angelic spirits, Lucifer. He abused his freedom and power and cried in rebellion, "I will not serve!" This moment of pride, crying, *I will be like God the Most High* (*Is.* 14:14), of looking to his own glory and power, was the moment of decision and the moment of rebellion. The tradition is that, at that time, his name was changed to Satan (the accuser) and the spiritual warfare was underway. Man would be the focal point of Satan's attack. Satan would then tempt our first parents with *you will be like gods* (*Gen.* 3:5), the same temptation to pride that caused his own downfall. And so the war continues against mankind.

A key point in this picture of the origin of evil spirits and of spiritual warfare, is that God created spirits with a share in His own freedom and power. Both the freedom and the power were misused, but God did not violate His own creation by destroying their freedom and power, or annihilating them. His choice was to win the victory by sending His Son to become one of us and win the battle in our flesh, crucified on the Cross.

Factors in the Spiritual Warfare

From this general reconstruction of events, we can see that there are several factors involved. First of all, we see God's merciful love and humility. In His merciful love, He created us after His own image and likeness, and in His humility, He showed the extent of the merciful love in redeeming us by becoming man and undergoing the humiliation of the passion and death on the cross for us.

The warfare carried on by Satan centers around whatever is associated with this Redemptive Incarnation of Christ, whatever has to do with humanity of Jesus and the extension of that humanity in the Church, His Body. This spiritual warfare centers around Mary, the Church, the Eucharist, the cross, humility and mercy, and our redeemed humanity.

Mary

Mary, in a special way, is the focal point of the spiritual warfare. Chosen by God to be mother of the Redeemer, she gives her own flesh to the Eternal Word, and God's merciful love and humility are incarnated in her womb. By her "yes," she becomes the mother of Jesus Christ Our Lord, and she continues that "yes" to become the Mother of Christ's Body, the Church. She is the new "Morning Star" and the Queen of Angels. It is her offspring that will crush the head of the serpent, with the heel for which Satan lies in wait. Uniquely, Mary, Mother of the Son of God and Mother of the Church, is at the center of this spiritual warfare.

In the main document of the Second Vatican Council, "The Constitution on the Church," the Church places Mary in its center (*Lumen Gentium,* 8). Mary is described as model, mother and queen: model of discipleship; mother of Jesus Christ and our mother; and queen, "exalted by the Lord as Queen of all, in order that she might be the more thoroughly conformed to her Son, the Lord of Lords and the conqueror of sin and death."

Mary has this same triple role in our regard: model, mother and queen. As model, she is a living example of what we are to be in this spiritual warfare—disciples to Jesus Christ, listening to the Word, pondering it in our hearts, yielding to it with a total surrender to the Holy Spirit, fulfilling perfectly the will of the Father. As mother of the Church, she has been chosen for us by God and commissioned to form us into the pattern of her Son Jesus, the Image of the Father, even to the pattern of His death (*See Phil.* 3:10) on the cross and so, His resurrection. And as queen, Mary, "the woman" of Revelation (*See Rev.* 12:1-2, 17), leads and guides us in this spiritual warfare.

The Church

Another focal point of spiritual warfare is the Church. The Church is the body of Christ and is the continuation of the Incarnation, and as such, is united in this struggle with Jesus as our Head.

The Church lives out the fundamental principle—like the Head, so the Body. Whatever happened in Jesus, our Head, is to happen in us, the Church. As He was born of Mary and the Holy Spirit, lived and worked by the Spirit, suffered, died and rose by the power of the Spirit, so we too are to follow this pattern. This means that as He confronted Satan, as He was lifted up on the Cross and was victorious, so we too confront Satan and will be victorious in Christ Jesus.

This monumental struggle is carried on in each and every person every day of our lives. The Church teaches this in the document, "The Church in the Modern World" stating:

> "For a monumental struggle against the powers of darkness pervades the whole history of man. The battle was joined from the very origins of the world and will continue until the last day, as the Lord has attested. Caught in this conflict, man is obliged to wrestle constantly if he is to cling to what is good. Nor can he achieve his own integrity without valiant efforts and the help of God's grace." (#37).

The Eucharist

At the heart of the Church is the Eucharist. John Paul II emphasizes that the Eucharist is above all else, a sacrifice.

"It is the sacrifice of the Redemption and also the sacrifice of the New Covenant. . . . Accordingly, precisely by making this single sacrifice present, man and the world are restored to God through the paschal newness of Redemption." (*Dominicae Cenae #9*).

It is this Sacrifice—Sacrament that applies Christ's victory to the warfare. The words of Jesus apply to this present moment: *Now has judgment come upon this world, now will this world's prince be driven out, and I—once I am lifted up from the earth—will draw all men to myself.* (*Jn.* 12:31, 32).

St. Ignatius of Antioch in his Letter to the Ephesians describes the power of the Eucharist in spiritual warfare:

"Try to gather together more frequently to celebrate God's Eucharist and to praise Him. For when you meet with frequency, Satan's powers are overthrown and his destructiveness is undone by the unanimity of your faith. There is nothing better than peace, by which all strife in Heaven and earth is done away."

The Sacrifice of the Eucharist applies the victorious power of the crucified and risen Christ to the here and now spiritual warfare.

The Cross of Christ

The Cross and Resurrection are God's chosen way for His Son, Jesus Christ. This mysterious path of death/resurrection is the way both for Jesus, our Head, and for us, His Body. The Cross is God's power and His wisdom and not man's. The way of the Cross is the way for the Church. The Calvary that the Church is currently experiencing is God's mysterious way at work, His power and wisdom, His victory in this spiritual warfare.

The Cross of Christ is very much illuminated in the spiritual warfare, because it's the full manifestation of God's mercy and humility. Hanging victoriously on the cross, suspended between Heaven and earth, Jesus is incarnate mercy; He is incarnate humility. It is this incarnate mercy and humility that defeats Satan and his angelic powers.

CHAPTER 6

RESPONSES TO SATAN'S TACTICS

Satan's tactics stand in direct opposition to the redemptive Incarnation and all that is part of it—Mary, Church, Eucharist, the Cross. His approach is one of pride and deception seeking to establish his own kingdom. Sacred Scripture and the Liturgy provide many passages that reveal Satan's tactics and attacks by capsulizing the contrast between the way of Christ and the way of Satan. They are like battle cries in this spiritual warfare, and can be used as a powerful response. I find that they become ejaculatory prayers in times of struggle and temptation. They are short and clear summaries of the Gospel that I can use to preach to myself in the daily battle.

Yours is the kingdom, the power and the glory, now and forever!
The *kingdom* is God's plan for the reign of Jesus as Lord of the whole universe. The *power* of God that raised Jesus from the dead will raise up our mortal bodies to reign with Him. The *glory* of the Father is Jesus, humble, obedient and exalted on the Cross, raised from the dead by the power of the Holy Spirit and now reigning. Mary's role as queen and mother is to prepare the Bride by way of the Cross for this glory, so that we may reign with Him.

Satan stands in direct opposition. He seeks the kingdom, the power and the glory. He is the great imitator and deceiver who wants to reign in our hearts through sin. He wants to be in charge. He tempts us to use our own power or his power, rather than the Holy Spirit's power that flows from Christ crucified and risen. Satan will use all of his power and deception to prevent a "second crucifixion," that is, the corporate crucifixion of the Body of Christ. He knows what happened when Jesus our Head was crucified! The crucifixion of the Church in humility and love will mean the final crushing of the head of Satan. Satan is pride, and seeks glory for himself in making us proud and rebellious.

I am the way, the truth and the life.

Jesus is the sole and unique *Way* to the Father. Jesus is the *Truth*, revealing the Father. Jesus is the *Life*, revealing the Father's love, making us sons and daughters with Him. The Second Vatican Council put it very clearly:

"The Church believes that Christ, Who died and was raised up for all (*See 2 Cor.* 5:15), can, through His Spirit, offer man the light and strength to measure up to his supreme destiny. Nor has any other name under Heaven been given to man by which it is fitting for him to be saved. (*See Acts* 4:12). She likewise holds that, in her most benign Lord and Master can be found the key, the focal point, and the goal of all human history." (*See Reference 4*).

Satan stands in direct opposition. Instead of being the Way, he is confusion, darkness and sin. Instead of being Truth, he is the liar that leads into error. Instead of being Life, he brings the fear of death and death itself. (*See Heb.* 2:15). The Second Vatican Council adds:

"But rather often, men deceived by the evil one, have become caught up in futile reasonings and have exchanged the truth of God for a lie, serving the creature rather than the Creator (*Cf. Rom.* 1:21-25), or some there are, who living and dying in a world without God, are subject to utter hopelessness." (*Lumen Gentium, #16*) (*See Reference 3*).

Jesus Christ is Lord!!

In this warfare we are under the leadership of Jesus Christ, Our Lord and Saviour. St. Ignatius of Loyola has pointed out that Christ's standard in this spiritual warfare is the way of poverty, love and humility. What a contrast to the world around us and to the Standard of Satan! Satan's way is the way of riches, honors and pride. The ways are clear and opposed to each other. Our choice must also be decisive and clear. Jesus Christ alone is Our Lord! No other lord must reign in our hearts. No riches, no honors, no pride, no sin and no self. Jesus alone must reign as Lord.

Stand Firm!

St. Paul, in his Letter to the Ephesians, describes the nature of the spiritual warfare—*Our battle is not against human forces but against the principalities and powers, the rulers of this world of darkness, the evil spirits in the region above.* (*Eph.* 6:12). He goes on to say that we must put on *God's armor* if we are to resist, hold our ground and stand firm. And God's armor is truth, justice, zeal, faith, salvation, the Word of God and prayer. This is the real armor and weaponry in spiritual warfare. This section of the Letter to the Ephesians forms a culmination of his whole letter. The text challenges us to "Stand firm in faith and fight with God's armor."

In contrast to God's armor is Satan's armor. Instead of God's gifts and virtues, we are presented with lies, error, confusion, pride, competitiveness, pleasure seeking, rationalizations, rebellious independence, empty words and hectic activity. All of these are calculated to promote our self-exaltation and thus, our defeat in this spiritual warfare.

The Kingdom of God is at hand. Repent and believe the good news! (*Mk.* 1:15).

The basic proclamation of the good news, calling for repentance and faith, is also the basic response to spiritual warfare: God's kingdom is here! Reform your lives, turn away from sin, and believe in Jesus, the Son of God! The key responses are faith in Jesus as Lord and a turning away from sin.

Sin is very much at issue. One of the targets of Satan, successful in our day, is the sin of impurity that binds us and prevents us from being fully the Body of Christ Incarnate. Impurity is of the heart, the mind, and the body, attacking our whole being. Impurity of the heart enthrones idols such as self, pride, materialism and self-reliance in our hearts. Impurity of mind clouds our minds with error and half-truths so that we are left in confusion. Impurity of body gives over our bodies to be temples of lust, rather than temples of the Holy Spirit.

Impurity is a special point in Satan's offensive because in this way he attacks the flesh that Jesus took on in the Incarnation, and sullies what is destined to be the Body of Christ. Impurity is a major area of spiritual warfare in our present day world—just look around!

Watch and pray!

To *"watch and pray"* is the often repeated exhortation of Jesus in times of temptation and trial (*Matt.* 24:42). This exhortation has been the basic teaching of the Church in regard to our preparedness and response for the time of temptation and trial. Daily we pray with the whole Church: *Deliver us from the evil one.* (*Matt.* 6:13). The ordained of the Church have continued to pray the Divine Office for all the members of the Church. Countless rosaries and ejaculations have been lifted up in intercession. But, above all, over 420,000 priests around the world offer the Eucharistic Body and Blood of the Lord Jesus Christ (an average of 8 to 10 thousand Masses at any given moment). The power of the Cross and Resurrection is being continually applied! The Church is continually ''watching and praying'' with the most effective remembrance of Christ's passion, death and resurrection, the Mass.

As the Second Vatican Council explains ''...the priest alone can complete the building up of the Body in the Eucharistic Sacrifice. Thus are fulfilled the words of God, spoken through His prophet: *From the rising of the sun even to the going down, my name is great among the Gentile, and in every place there is sacrifice, and there is offered to my name a clean oblation.* (*Mal.* 1:11). In this way, the Church simultaneously prays and labors in order that the entire world may become the People of God, the Body of the Lord...'' *(See Reference 3)*.

In direct contrast to this approach is that of Satan who tempts us not to watch and pray. He tempts us to say to ourselves, like the rich man in the gospel, *You have blessings in reserve for years to come. Relax! Eat heartily, drink well. Enjoy yourself.* (*Lk.* 12:19). But we know the answer: *You fool! This night your life will be required of you. To whom will all this piled-up wealth of yours go?* (*Lk.* 12:20).

Rejoice, Christ Crucified is Risen!

Christ crucified and risen is our victory! Rejoice! What has happened to Christ Jesus is to happen to us. We are to follow His steps to victory. And this is a real point of attack for Satan. He does not want us to "move on" as described in the Letter to the Hebrews, Chapter 5 and 6. Satan wants to prevent us from "moving on" to the maturity of victim-intercession. He wants to prevent another crucifixion at any cost. The crucifixion of Christ's Body, the Church, will mean the final completion of the warfare. We experience Satan's attacks by his temptations to stay where we are, not to "move on." We experience fears of death (*Heb.* 2:15) and fears of the Cross. We take our eyes off our victorious Lord and look to our weakness and fears. This is Satan's tactic. The battle cry of the Christian, however, is "Look to Jesus!" "Look to Christ Crucified and Risen! Rejoice for the accuser of our brothers is cast out!" The tomb is empty!

What Can We Do Individually?

What can we do in our daily living to enter into the "power and wisdom of God" and apply the victory given to us in Mary, the Church, the Eucharist and the Cross?

We can entrust our lives and ministry to **Mary**, consecrate our lives to her, and thus invite and allow her to be mother, forming us daily into the pattern of Christ and let her be queen, to lead and guide us in this spiritual warfare.

We can be more fully **Church** by our love, reverence, service and submission to the hierarchy and people established by God. Through an obedient faith flows the unity Jesus prayed for the night before He died.

We can live a **Eucharistic** life more fully by frequent, even daily, offering of the Eucharistic Sacrifice. Each time we offer the Eucharist, we remember and apply the victorious passion, death and resurrection of Jesus Christ Our Lord until He comes in glory.

We can live a **crucified life**, offering all our suffering with love, in union with the Eucharistic Lord for the salvation of all. God's love, poured into our hearts, transforms suffering into joy. The Cross is the "power and wisdom of God" applied to this present spiritual warfare. Our sufferings offered with love for the salvation of others are so precious we must not waste them. We can use all sufferings to apply Christ's victory in this spiritual warfare.

We can actually rejoice in the battle, because when we are "hassled" by Satan, it means that we are standing in the right place—with our heel crushing his head. We need to stand firm in our faith and enjoy the fight.

We can always practice mercy and humility. These are God's ways. They are like universal laws that cannot be broken. God is always merciful, and God exalts the humble. Mercy and humility are the most effective weapons against Satan, because they directly oppose the stance of Satan.

We can use all the armor of God and pray the great battle cries:

> "Yours is the kingdom, the power and the glory, now and forever!"
> "Jesus, the way, the truth and the life."
> "Jesus Christ is Lord!"
> "The kingdom of God is at hand, repent and believe the good news!"
> "Watch and pray!"
> "Rejoice! Christ crucified is risen!"

What Can We As Church Do?

The most effective thing we can do, as Church, is to be **fully Church**. To be fully Church means to live the mission of the Church, the mission of the Victorious Christ. It means to be in "labor" at the Cross of the broken body of Christ, and likewise to pray as a united Body in the Cenacle, that the whole world may become the People of God, the Body of the Lord, the temple of the Holy Spirit. (*Lumen Gentium* #17). To be fully Church involves both the *Cross* and the *Cencacle*. It is through these two events that the Church is born and it is through these two events that the Church is victorious in its spiritual warfare.

Because the Church is the focal site of spiritual warfare, the Church must be aware of who she is and whom she is battling. The Church's power is in the power of the Cross and the power of Pentecost, the Cenacle.

The Power of the Cross

The crucifixion and death of Christ Jesus is not just an historical event that happened once, but is an event that continues to happen now in His "Broken Body." It is happening in us, His suffering Body, now. The victory won for us by Jesus, our Head, is now being applied to the whole world through the redemptive suffering of His Church. Here is the victory in this spiritual warfare. What happened in and through Jesus is now happening to us. It is a time of corporate Calvary bringing redemption to the whole world.

As Church, we need wisdom to understand the Cross and love to embrace the cross of Christ for the sake of others. If we don't have this kind of wisdom and love of the Cross, we need to ask for it in prayer. This wisdom and love is the source of God's own victorious power. It is only with this wisdom and love that we will be able to embrace the Cross for others with peace and joy. It is then we can rejoice with the heavens because *the accuser of our brothers is cast out— defeated by the blood of the Lamb and by the word of their testimony.* (Rev. 12:11).

At the Cross, we, the Church, need to stand firm as Mary did, because Satan continues *to make war on the rest of her offspring, on those who keep God's commandments and give witness to Jesus* (Rev. 12:17). Like Jesus, we have Mary to support us and intercede for us in this time of spiritual warfare. So we really need to live entrusted to her, as Jesus requested of us from the Cross so that she may carry out her motherly role.

In daily practice, we as Church, can stand at the Cross of Jesus with Mary our Mother and implore God's mercy: "For the sake of His sorrowful Passion, have mercy on us and on the whole world." *(Mercy of God chaplet).*

The Power of a Cenacle

The power of the Cross prepares us and purifies us for the *Cenacle.* A Cenacle is the place of united intercessory prayer for the outpouring of the Holy Spirit. The work of the Cenacle is a united work, and so the necessary preparation for it is through the purification of the Cross. We enter the Cenacle by way of the Cross; we enter following the path of Jesus.

A Cenacle is located wherever the Church gathers in unity, purified by the Cross. It is a gathering of unity of heart and mind together with Mary, the Mother of Jesus, and Peter and the Apostles (*See Acts* 1:14). It is in this unity and from this unity, that the Church can most effectively intercede for the outpouring of the Holy Spirit and for the coming of the Lord Jesus Christ. In the Cenacle, the Church is most fully Church, because here it cries out as Bride of Christ, in union with the Holy Spirit, "Come, Lord Jesus!" When enough members of the Church gather united in a Cenacle and cry out for the coming of the Lord, He will, in fact, come!

In each profession of faith, in every "Our Father" prayed, in each Eucharist offered, we cry out for the coming of the Lord. His coming will be a time of His reigning in our hearts. It will be a time of His kingdom when all will know Jesus as Lord, and Bridegroom to the glory of the Father.

CHAPTER 7

SPIRITUAL WARFARE AND THE RENEWAL MOVEMENTS OF THE CHURCH

Renewal movements of the Church are also a special point of attack. Satan's goal of course, is to prevent the truth of the renewal movement message from reaching the majority in the Church. Satan must use the weaknesses of these movements to hinder the important truths that they are to convey. The result is that the truth of their movements is not heard, and in fact, cannot be heard because so many other contradictory messages are being broadcast simultaneously.

It is important for the members and especially leaders of renewal movements to understand the weaknesses in these movements. It is the weaknesses that are often being broadcast as the message, and the truth is effectively blocked. Ignoring a weakness or being unaware of Satan's presence, leaders become ineffective, or even confuse the direction of the renewal.

Charismatic Renewal

As an example, the charismatic renewal in the Church can be studied from this angle. Over the last decade and a half since the charismatic renewal has been present within the Catholic Church, two types of messages have been widely broadcast—one the truth in its context, and the other the reality of its own weaknesses. The *truth* of that message is very important to the renewal of the Church, for it reveals the wonderful effects of being baptized in the Holy Spirit. In the light of this truth, we see people coming to know Jesus as their personal Lord and Saviour, coming to recognize God

51

as their Father through the power of the Holy Spirit, and we witness them experiencing and using the charismatic gifts of the Holy Spirit to build up the Body of Christ. We recognize that the truth in this message is really the truth of the Gospel itself, and needs to be made known to the whole Church.

The other message being broadcast, however, is a message arising from the weaknesses of the members of the renewal. It is a voice that periodically speaks of division, party splits, factions, rivalaries, distortion of truth, self-righteousness, jealousies, and sins of lust or worldly avarice. What confuses the listener is the fact that two different messages are being broadcast simultaneously by the same people. It is through such confusion and distortion that Satan wins his battle.

The very truth that a renewal movement is meant to convey, often becomes the source of its weakness because of distortion of the truth. It is a distortion where one truth is chosen to the neglect of others. On the other hand, a truth can also be so boxed in, ignored, and hedged in by excuses or rationalization, that it does not reach the vast majority of the Church. All of this is part of the tactics of Satan, and there are many examples. The recognition and acceptance of the baptism in the Holy Spirit can be so hemmed in by misunderstandings, that it is not accepted as an experience available to all, and is considered as not needed by the whole Church. On the other hand, it can be made so central a truth that sacramental Baptism and Confirmation are considered secondary or non-essential. The various gifts of the Holy Spirit can suffer similar neglect or distortion. The gift of tongues for the upbuilding of faith can be ignored as irrelevant babble, or distorted by considering it as **the** sign of baptism in the Spirit. The gift of prophecy can be ignored by Church leaders, or made so exclusive a channel of God's word that the Magesterium leadership and teachings are ignored. The Sacred Scriptures can be so analyzed that they no longer serve as God's word of salvation, or so distorted by private interpretation and fundamentalism, that they become only a caricature of God's word. Even the gift of discernment of spirits can be replaced by reasonings and parliamentary procedure or, on the other hand, seen as so exclusive a property of those in the charismatic renewal, that they consider themselves the only direct pipeline to God.

All these tactics of blockage and distortion are the work of Satan to prevent the truth of renewal movements from reaching the heart of the Church. The leaders of renewal have a serious obligation to look at the strengths and weaknesses of their renewal, and to examine their own process of discernment to make certain that, they in fact, are hearing the word of the Lord. They need to ask themselves:

> "What spirit is at work among us? The Holy Spirit, human spirits or the evil spirits?"
> "What is the Holy Spirit telling us today?"
> "What is the Holy Spirit telling the Church? The Holy Father? The Magisterium and the conferences of Bishops?"
> "Are we hearing the word of the Holy Father on the condition of the Church and the world? Are we hearing his call to respond to this condition with mercy and consecration to Mary?"
> "Are we hearing the truth of other complementary renewal movements, or are we experiencing the blockage and distortion of Satan's tactics? For example, are we just hearing about Mary from Marian movements? Are we hearing the cry for social reforms from social movements?"
> "Are we pointing the finger of judgment at others while forgetting the plank in our own eyes?"
> "Are we complaining about being considered on the fringes of the Church, and yet have not heard the truth proclaimed by the Church on what it means to be in the heart of the Church?"
> "Are we trapped in our pride, our own self-righteousness, our own capabilities?"

These are examples of the kinds of questions leaders need to ask of themselves to truly discern the movement of the

Holy Spirit against a tactic of Satan hindering the truth of the renewal movements.

On the part of the general laity of the charismatic renewal, there are also obstacles and weaknesses that prevent the truth of the message being heard. In the past, many have ridiculed Pentecostals as "holy rollers," "snake charmers," or "emotional fanatics." This kind of ridicule has made it impossible for them to hear the truth of the message. Much of this ridicule continues today. Others are bound by their own problems of practical atheism, rationalism, or secularism, and they are unable to hear any channel of input other than the single channel they are tuned in on. In this way Satan has won another battle, sealing the ears of the listeners.

Satan's efforts against renewal movements are very effective in distorting communication. Fortunately, however, the general strategy of Satan is also exposed by his attacks, and we can learn from this.

The central strategy of Satan's attack is against the **unity** of the movement. He actively seeks to destroy the unity of leaders and members. In this way, he attacks the unity for which Jesus prayed the night before he died. This tactic of Satan is one that is common to all warfare: "Divide and conquer." There are a variety of ways he uses to divide—attacks on unity itself, on the unity of the truth of the message, on the humility of the members of the renewal, and on the integrity of the personal lives of the members, especially its leaders. The result is division within, and a separation from the heart of the Church. The attack "pigeon-holes" the renewal into a slot that makes it ineffective. It sets boundaries around the renewal so that its message is isolated. Another result is limited cooperation among leaders, and other complementary movements. A message of disunity is louder than the message of the truth of the renewal.

Satan also directly attacks the **truth** and thus fosters disunity. The "father of lies" confuses with half-truths, distortions, distraction from the issues at hand. It could be said that if Satan cannot prevent a parade, then he will lead it. The "father of lies" is not against using little lies, nor against using the "big lie"—that is, a lie so big that many believe it.

He also attacks **humility** with pride. Pride comes from the very nature of Satan's being. He causes great disunity by tempting us to a similar stance of pride, pride of having us center on ourselves. Our lives then become self-fulfilling, self-centered, self-glorifying, self-sufficient. He urges us to use our strengths and capabilities as though they were our own, instead of recognizing that they are gifts from God. Thus our very strengths become weaknesses instead. He divides members (and especially leaders), by accusations, jealousies, competition and rivalries. He leads us to ridicule a childlike spirit. He leads us to disdain submission and any form of humility. Does this have a "new age" ring to it?

The devil also attacks the **integrity** of the personal lives of leaders. If he can undermine a leader, he can cause confusion and disunity. Since leaders affect so many of the members, they are a special point of attack. Satan tempts all of us (but especially leaders), with sins of the flesh and attachments to a worldly spirit, and to worldy goods.

To each of these tactics against unity, truth, humility, and integrity, Satan adds **fear**. With fear he can paralyze us, preventing us from acting and using the gifts God has given us. Fear stirs up feelings within us that inhibit our free action, feelings of inadequacy. In a sense, fear withdraws the very oxygen we need to breathe, and so we suffocate. Jesus, however, came to free us from the bondage of fear. It is His perfect love that casts out all fear. (*See 1 Jn.* 5:18).

Strategy of Defense

The strategy of defense against the tactics of Satan is knowledge of the truth and a commitment to that truth. This type of knowledge is necessary and vital to the strength of the charismatic renewal movement.

1. Knowledge of the *reality* of spiritual warfare.

Spiritual warfare is something real. It cannot be ignored as though it didn't exist, or that it will go away by itself. Such crass ignorance gives the victory to Satan. The "Book of Revelation" opens the curtain to spiritual warfare, and describes the reality of the battle between Jesus and Satan.

2. Knowledge of the *victory* of Jesus alone.
    Jesus is the victor over Satan, sin and death by His redemptive Incarnation. He further emptied Himself in humble obedience by dying for us on the cross. His resurrection by the Holy Spirit won for Him the victory.
    Each one of us, as members of His Body, the Church, are to share in this victory by following in His footsteps. We have been given authority over Satan and can use the power of the name of Jesus in that regard. Whenever we are harried by Satan, in any of the areas of unity, truth, humility, integrity or fear, we can take the spiritual authority given us and say in simple faith:

> "In the name of Jesus and by the power of
> His precious Blood I take authority over you
> (Satan, spirit of confusion, of lies, of lust, . . .
> etc.) and order you to be gone, bound to Jesus."

The victory of Jesus has been given to His Church. We can use freely what has been given freely.

3. Knowledge of Mary as mother and queen by *consecration*.
    Mary is God's choice for His Son and for us. She assures us of the Incarnation by providing flesh for the Word of God to become Jesus. God's plan is that we are to follow in His way of humility and mercy, the way of the cross and resurrection, and so victory. Specifically, Mary's role is to prepare us for the cross by teaching us. Consecration to Mary allows her to prepare us. It is our "fiat."
    Satan seems to delight, in a special way, in blocking the role of Mary, the humble woman who gave flesh to Jesus. She was the starting point for his total defeat. Now, as Mary is bringing that victory to completion in us, we see his obvious assault on blocking Mary's messages.
    The response is to live totally entrusted to Mary, as her little ones so that as "her heel" we can crush the head of Satan in our own lives.

4. Knowledge of the *point* of attack.

The attack of Satan is focused most effectively on the "power points," the leaders, the ordained, especially on the hierarchy who are the leaders of worship. The priests have been very much the point of attack by Satan, because they are the celebrants of the Eucharist, which is the summit and source of unity.

In recent years Satan has been effective in attacking priests in general, and priests in the charismatic renewal. This can be clearly seen in the disunity among priests and bishops, confusion over the truth of the Church's teaching on faith and morals, pride in self-fulfillment and self-reliance, loss of personal integrity through sins of lust and avarice, and a loss of devotion to Mary in the lives of many.

5. Knowledge of the *Holy Spirit*: discernment.

Knowledge of the Holy Spirit and discernment of His word and action are absolutely essential to renewal. We need to seek out what the Spirit is saying to the Church and what the Spirit is saying to the renewal.

When we can "see and hear" the Spirit in the Church and in our lives, we will be given eyes and ears to see and hear what the Spirit is saying in Sacred Scripture.

Discernment is the gift of gifts, because by it we recognize the presence and action of the Holy Spirit, and, what is not of the Holy Spirit; namely, our own human spirit or the evil spirit.

6. Knowledge of the *timing* of the Lord.

God's time is different from ours. His is eternity. An awareness of His Lordship over time and a radical trust in Him are essential for renewal movements. An example from the Old Testament is His timing in the life of Joseph. The young dreamer was attacked by his brothers and sold as a slave into Egypt, where in God's perfect way, and in His perfect timing, Joseph was raised up as the provider and saviour of his brothers.

For God, all is present as an eternal "now." We need the patient perseverance to wait upon the Lord's perfect timing.

Other Renewal Movements

The charismatic renewal is only one of many renewals. But the same tactics of Satan are at work in all renewals, and so the knowledge of the strategy of defense must be part of the equipment of all leaders.

The great increase in communities, in prayer groups, in extended participation of the laity in the function of the parish, and in evangalization, all such movements and actions are included. As such, they are included as targets by Satan as well.

CHAPTER 8

ANOTHER TARGET: COMMUNITIES

Those who work to form community have no doubts that Satan is working against their efforts. Communities are a vital target because Satan knows the power of two or three who gather in the name of the Lord *(See Matt. 18:19-20)*. Satan attacks any and all communities: families, prayer and sharing groups, rectory and convent households, covenant communities, and religious orders and congregations. His tactic is to prevent unity of heart and mind in the relationships of the members. To the extent that Satan can disrupt the good relationships within a community, he achieves a victory against the Lord's desire that we be one in heart and mind. To the extent that the community is divided, the Body of Christ is broken and Satan achieves his purpose.

It is important to understand how he goes about this so that we may respond with the appropriate strategy of defense. An attack against unity is primarily an attack on the relationships of the members, but he does not neglect efforts against the truth of the situation, and against the humility and integrity of the members.

Expect Satan to tempt us to judge one another. We then grow impatient and critical when differences "grind" on each other, supplying fuel to make little disputes into confrontations. He can activate our imagination to conjure up whole court scenes, as we "nurse and rehearse" what we imagine to be the situation, reviewing what we think we should have said or will say. We end up "accusing the brethren," falling into the trap of the devil whose very name means "the accuser."

Through a variety of such tactics Satan can snatch away the word of God given to us regarding our relationships: *Love one another as I love you.*

The "awareness" of the very fact that our relationships are being attacked by Satan is already a tremendous step in making an effective defense. Satan will spare no effort in using all his ingenious cleverness to tempt us in our relationships. Fortunately, the more vivid the temptation, the easier it is to recognize, especially if the temptation suddenly brings things to our memory, out of nowhere, such as past injustices and hurts. You can be sure that he is hard at work, trying his best to distract and to disrupt. As we will reflect on later, one response to these kinds of temptations is to rejoice, to thank and praise God for His mercy, His Incarnation. Really, we can simply laugh at the efforts of Satan in trying to disrupt relationships.

The evil one must also attack the **truth**. It can easily happen that the truth of existing situations is confused by misinterpretations, or facts and decisions that are not clearly and fully communicated. Confusion can easily grow. Suspicions, jealousies, judgments and rumors only increase the confusion. Truth is something very precious, and needs to be protected by silence in certain situations. Silence is often called for in response to rumors, accusations, and to confidential and privileged information. Silence is also a necessary response to accusations arising from jealousies and hatred.

In other situations, we need to protect the truth and avoid confusion, by "speaking the truth in love." This can be even more difficult than keeping silent, especially for the one who does the speaking. We need to emphasize both truth and love. We cannot speak just the "truth" alone, as often happens when we speak in sinful anger or without love. Nor can we speak only "in love," without truth, because this is a form of flattery that compounds the confusion. "Speaking the truth in love" is a way of bringing confusion out of the dark and into the light. It is exposing the situation, as it is, to the light of Christ. Realize that Satan will always try to keep the truth of a situation under a dark cloud of confusion.

Thus we fall into his temptations of speaking when we should be silent, and of remaining silent when we should be speaking. Truth that remains under a cloud of confusion fosters strained relationships.

As mentioned in the previous chapter on renewal, there is always attack against **humility**. He tempts us to pride which matures into jealousy and envy. He offers us a variety of forms of pride: prestige of honors and position, power in control over others, possession of material goods, and possession of gifts and talents. When pride reigns in the hearts of the members and leaders of communities, then there is no room for humility, no room for submission to one another, and eventually, no room for real leadership and authority. With pride, there is no possibility for unity of heart and mind, and no possibility of humble service.

How easy it is for us in community to go the way of pride—to stand on our rights, to take offense at the corrections given by others, to defend and excuse our wrong-doing, to pout and go off into a corner to lick our wounds. The response to pride is humility, but who of us hears the call: *Learn of Me because I am meek and humble of heart?* Humility is the good soil in which community can grow to maturity and produce its harvest.

In close proximity, Satan also attacks our unity by attacking our personal integrity. If one member is wounded, all of us are wounded. Satan knows well that soil that is good—well plowed and fertilized—can produce weeds even better than good seed. The better the soil, the better the weeds grow! Thus, the more members of communities grow spiritually, the more they need to be attentive to weeds. The weeds of Satan are obvious: pride, avarice, lust and the attachment to worldly ways. The weed of impurity, in a special way, can take over the whole of the garden, that is, the impurity of heart and mind as well as of body. The heart is impure when drawn to attachments other than the Lord; the mind is impure when contaminated with novel teachings; the body is impure when given to lustful desires and relations. St. Paul, in writing to the Churches he founded, regularly warns against the disunity that enters a community when sin invades the personal lives of its members. As the dark cloud over all of this, Satan brings fear and sadness. Fears arise to paralyze the community: fears of what others think, fears of how others will respond, fears of inadequacy, and general fears of unknown origin. Sadness, too, (such as over-seriousness), weighs heavily on the hearts of the community members. Sadness means no joy and no rejoicing, so that the community is not a witness to the Risen Lord Jesus, not a center of hope.

So how do we handle this? A good response should include several factors. It includes the very basic elements of Christian life, with a focus on the unity of heart and mind. We review them here:

- A deeper *commitment* to the Lord Jesus through deeper conversion of our lives and ministry to Him, and a deeper surrendering to His Holy Spirit.

- A living *consecration* to our Blessed Mother so that she may form us into the perfect image of her Son, and prepare us for spiritual warfare through a greater docility.

- A life of humble obedience to, and reverence for, the *Church*. An attitude of submission to the Church is one of the great defenses against Satan. Obedience and humility directly counter his attacks. We can never go wrong by obedience to the Church— even if at the time we may think that it would be more reasonable to follow another course. Obedience is better than sacrifice. This obedience and reverence is expressed toward the Pope and the bishops in union with him. Such humble obedience and submission also needs to be part of relationships within the community itself. Each member is a unique member of the body that needs to act in unity of heart and mind.

- A life of *confession*, confessing the two-fold reality that Jesus is Lord and we are sinners. When Jesus is proclaimed as Lord in the community both individually and communally, and when we forgive one another and ask for forgiveness of the Lord and one another, both privately and publicly, then we have community, and Satan has no foothold among us. Sin will always be with us, so we always need forgiveness, and it is always available where Jesus is Lord and Saviour. To the extent we have forgiveness, we have community.

• Clear channels of *communication*. Clear and regular communication allows sharing and exchange, not only of information, but also of concerns and needs. Sharing is of the very nature of community: sharing of our lives, our goals, our talents, our faith and our love. Clear and regular sharing is an effective antidote against Satan's poisonous attacks against the communication within community. Trouble is under way when members stop talking and sharing to one another.

• Regular *prayer*. We need to ask for the grace of unity of heart and mind, the grace of community. In a word, we need to pray. Only with God's love can we love one another with the commitment of brothers and sisters in the Lord. This love is a gift of His Holy Spirit and He has requested us to ask for it: *God's love has been poured into our hearts through the Holy Spirit who has been given to us. (RSV Rom. 5:5).* But we need to ask: "So I say to you, 'Ask and you shall receive'. . . how much more will the heavenly Father give the Holy Spirit to those who ask him." *(Lk. 11:9-13).* It is only the Holy Spirit that makes us one.

As we pray for one another, we bless one another with God's love, given by His Spirit that makes us one. When the Spirit of God dwells in our hearts, no evil spirits can dwell there. The kingdom of God has come.

• Taking *spiritual authority*. We have been given power over snakes and scorpions *(See Lk. 10:19)*, and when we discern the presence of evil spirits attacking community, we have the authority to cast them out. There is great power in the united prayer of community. We need to better utilize it.

• *Cooperation* in works of mercy binds a community in humble service. This is the attitude of Christ. Working together in works of service for others binds together the hearts of those working. A common apostolic work has been the founding charism of many religious communities and made them strong against the attacks of the Evil One.

• A life of *discipline*. To be strong against the attacks of Satan, we need to watch as well as pray. Ascetical practices have been part of the Church's armor: prayer, vigils, fasting, mortification, and penances. All of these strengthen our stand of faith and also make reparation and atonement for our sins as a community and for the sins of the world. But other forms of discipline are also needed in our modern times, the most needed being an ordered life. So many of our lives need restructuring in the use of our time, the priority of commitments, and in submission to authority over us. Satan delights in a disordered life which has no time for prayer, no time for study, and no time for works of mercy.

• The virtue of *patience*. Patience is a particularly necessary virtue for the life of community. We need patience with each other's human foibles, patience with daily differences and tensions. St. Paul tells us that the first characteristic of love is patience. *Love is patient.* (*1 Cor.* 13:4). The literal translation of the Greek is very much more to the point: "Love is long-suffering." To live with each other means we will "suffer long." This kind of patience is part of our humanity and is the very "stuff" of which love is made. What is dealt with in "speaking the truth in love" is sin and wrong doing.

- The gift of *rejoicing*! Rejoicing is the Christian response to spiritual warfare because we know we have the victory in Christ Jesus. An abiding ability to rejoice should be a characteristic of Christian communities. Rejoicing in the Lord dispels fears and sadness brought on by Satan's efforts. Rejoicing is an expression of trust in the Lord.

So rejoice you heavens, the accuser of our brothers is cast out. (*Rev.* 12:10-12).

CHAPTER 9

SATAN AND THE FAMILY

The concerted attacks of Satan are seen to have their most devastating effects on the families of our age. Family life is being decimated, and many are already destroyed. I do not need to look far for signs of Satan's attacks and none of us need statistics to prove that the family is under attack. In many of our families and those of our relatives, we can cite examples of every kind: divorce, separation, adultery, cohabitation, pre-marital sex and pregnancies outside of marriage, and abortion. Each of us can give our own sad story—and there is more. These situations are aggravated by alcohol, drugs, pornography, money, the mass media message of secularism and materialism.

The children are the ones who suffer the most. The results find our young with a lack of security, confused identity and role models, loss of commitment, high rate of drug use, sexual promiscuity and teen-age suicide. They are compounded by strong peer pressures, values inculcated by the secular schools and mass media, and the brain-washing of rock music.

Recently, I heard mention of a statistic that stated that almost 50% of the children in elementary school come from single parent homes. That is both incredible and frightening, and pinpoints much of the blame for much of the problem with youth today.

The results have an effect on all of us—sadness, confusion, depression, anger, and a host of pneumo-psychosomatic diseases. Our defenses are weakened and we can be overcome with diseases even such as cancer, arthritis and heart disorders.

The family, as the basic unit of society, is under a multilateral attack of all the forces of Hell itself, resulting in confusion, disunity, glorification of the flesh and pleasure. These three areas include a majority of the problems that I'll comment on in terms of spiritual warfare.

Confusion

As stated, Satan is the father of lies. His specialty is to confuse our minds and what an effective job he has done on the value system of the world! He has made use of the mass media to establish an environment of a secularism and materialism that has polluted the very air we breathe. We are gradually suffocating without being aware of it.

A particular area of confusion that he has promoted is the confusion of the roles of men and women as fathers and mothers of families. Not only are the parents confused, but the children are confused, because their models are confused.

Once we have set aside faith and hope in Jesus Christ, then love also becomes confused and becomes identified with sexual pleasure only. Respect for the God-given power of procreation is gone, and so too is the respect for life. Only in Jesus Christ do we find truth and without Him there is confusion.

Disunity

Another powerful attack is against the unity of the family. The attack against mutual relationships is obvious—lack of communication and sharing, resentments, jealousies, judgments, anger, unfaithfulness, separation and divorce. So many of these kinds of disorders are not just psychological—there is sin involved and the sin needs to be dealt with as sin, by forgiveness, repentance, the Sacrament of Reconciliation, prayer for healing, and deliverance. Disorders are not merely psychological or sociological problems that can be solved by better communication. Certainly better communication is needed but also the admission of sin. Sin is the great obstacle to peace and unity in the family. Where there is sin, there is no unity of heart or mind.

Thanks be to God that sin is something that can be dealt

with by turning to the merciful Saviour. Sin is bad enough, but what is even worse is not turning to the mercy of the Lord, and to one another, and asking for mercy. We will only find peace when we repent and turn to the Lord for His mercy.

The warfare against the unity of the marriage bond is made even more devasting by the world's view of marital relationships. In contrast to the world view, spouses cannot supply all the needs and wants of their partners. Only an intimate union with the Lord can provide all our needs. A false or exaggerated expectancy of what a spouse is capable of, aggravates the strained relationship.

Glorification of the Flesh and Pleasure

Our current society sees a great need to exaggerate the pleasures of the flesh. Much like Eve in the garden of Eden, we too are tempted to see and imagine the pleasure in what God has forbidden. The most effective way Satan has attacked us in this area is to separate sex from procreation. By condoning masturbation, abortion, adultery, and artificial birth control, the God-given use of sex is separated from procreation and sought for mutual or self pleasure only.

The pleasure of sex separated from the life-giving process is extolled in the mass media and by easily available pornography. The peer-pressure of the secular society has made this all the harder on the teenagers of this generation.

What Defenses Do We Have?

- Label secularism for what it is and stand against it. Say "No!"
- Unite with families of like mind and heart.
- Label SIN for what it is, and repent and forgive.
- Honor virginity as a preparation for marriage and for celibate life alike.
- Honor the marriage bed because sex is holy and marriage is a sacrament.

- Call on the mercy of the Lord for help and forgiveness.

- Call on the Holy Family for help: Jesus for Mercy, Mary for purity, and Joseph for steadfast righteousness before the Lord.

- Pray, as a family, and for your family, everyday.

- Strive to look beneath the surface of the phony, artificial promises of the world (Satan), in favor of lasting virtues of friendship, honor, peace and love.

- Spend one minute each day concentrating on what is at stake—your soul!

CHAPTER 10

AND AGAINST THE YOUTH

What has happened to the youth? What family, what parent, what pastor has not seen and experienced the anguish of our youth? We see a generation that has been kidnapped, by a culture that is anti-Christian.

Recently, the lay Catholic community called *Servants of Christ the King* in Steubenville, Ohio, numbering 330 adults and 205 children, held a conference on the "Attack against Youth." By a series of teachings, fiim and TV clips, and discussions, the pastoral leaders of the community raised the awareness level of the situation. This was the first step to a major program of study and action in response to the massive problem.

Statistics of the youth culture are alarming. The youth population in the United States, under 25 years old, is over 90 million (40% of the total), and this is the generation that has been stolen from us as evidenced by statistics on the media, sex, money, and suicide:

Media

• Youth watch an average of 26 hours of TV a week.
  (People of Destiny, 1/86).

• The total average of exposure to the electronic media is 60 to 70 hours a week.

• MTV goes to over 24 million homes.

• Teens who watch MTV average over an hour a day.
  (Rolling Stone, 12/8/83).

- Rock music is currently a 15 billion dollar industry. Its gross income surpasses that of professional sports, motion picture and television industries combined! (*People of Destiny,* 1/86).

The top ten road shows grossed an income of 190 million dollars in 1985 from concerts alone.

Sex

- Percentage of girls admitting to having sexual intercourse: 15-year-olds 20%, 17-year-olds 40%. (*Time,* 12/9/85).

- Teen pregnancy rate in United States is 95 per 1,000, 45% ending in abortion.

Money

- The estimated annual spending of girls under 20 years old is 30 billion a year. (*Wall Street Journal,* 11/9/84).

- American girls under 20 years old spent 8.4 billion dollars in preparation for the 1984-85 school year. (*Business Week,* 8/19/85).

Suicide

- In the United States, in 1984, there were close to 6,500 suicides between 15- and 24-year-olds (one every 1-1/2 hours).

- The suicide rate among the 15-19-year-olds has increased 300% in the last 30 years.

These are only some of the statistics that show the tip of the iceberg. Today (1990), the problem is much greater. We are dealing with a stolen generation, stolen by a Satanic strategy that has been very effective. Here is some of the strategy used by Satan, as presented at the "Attack on Youth" conference:

- Isolate the youth from parents and authority by fostering rebellion against all authority, especially parents.

- Take control of the youth world by dominating the youth culture carriers; namely, the school, the media, (especially the electronic media), and the peer group.

- Pump the youth full of hellish doctrine.

- Use the youth culture to evangelize the wider adult culture.

- Export this culture to the rest of the world.

The whole of this strategy is based on the "big lie," so effectively used by Adolph Hitler, who held that if the lie is big enough and absurd enough, it will be believed. This "big lie" can be seen in the characteristics of the youth culture. It is a world that is isolated and enclosed, focused on the now with little concern for the future. The measures for one being considered a success are based on such unimportant characteristics as looks and popularity. It is a culture that is profoundly self-centered, asking whether "I am happy and having fun." It means that relationships are shallow, with lots of mistrust and facades. The result is a double life—one with adults, and another with peers. And so parents appear dull, stupid and unreasonable. This whole culture has a strong commercial basis. The most unfortunate characteristic of the youth culture is that it is a big lie. It doesn't work, as seen by the number of suicides and the amount of depression, laced with chemical dependency.

The "Attack on Youth" conference dealt with rock music in a special way because it is the vehicle of the youth culture. Rock and youth culture are almost synonymous. Rock, in its rhythm, in its body language and in its lyrics, proclaims the themes of sex, rebellion, Satan, death, drugs and anti-Christianity—at times blatantly and other times subtly. Rock is an emotional experience of transcendence, and the rock concert is a liturgy.

The difficult and sensitive question of so-called "Christian Rock" needs to be carefully evaluated. Does rock music with Christian lyrics baptize rock, or does it subtly expose the youth to a dangerous habit? What is contemporary Christian music? What is its effect?

The influence of rock has become widespread throughout the world. Significant dates of development show its rapid growth:

1950 Transistor radios became readily available.
1951 TV use becomes widespread in the United States.
1954 Elvis Presley and the rise of Rock.
1964 The Beatles take Rock to the masses.
1969 Rock and revolution are wedded at the Woodstock concert.
1981 MTV comes on the scene.

In addition to rock music, movies and pornographic magazines have been evangelizing by means of sex and rebellion. The blatant attack on our youth follows the same pattern Satan used against our first parents—Rebellion and promises of grandeur. The big lie!

Unfortunately, the youth of the United States are not the only ones being attacked. Youth around the world are being bombarded in a massive strategy of sex and rebellion. I was struck by the fact that sex and rebellion are the predominant evangelistic tools. They are in direct contrast to the message of Mary, crying out for her children: "Be pure, be humble." Again, we can see the work of Satan as an attack on the woman and *her offspring, on those who keep God's commandments and give witness to Jesus.* (*Rev.* 12:17).

The attack on youth is the most devastating because it affects the next generation. It is a radical secularism that makes the youth proclaim, "God, I don't need You!" in a discordant echo of the cry of Lucifer, "I will not serve!" We need to be aware of this in order to respond. This was the first step of the strategy of response to the lay community of *Servants of Christ the King,* in presenting the conference on the "Attack on Youth."

The first response is, rightly, the awareness of Satan's existence and strategy. But then what? This is the challenge taken on by the community at Steubenville, among others. Additional conferences will be devoted to teaching on parental authority and the honor due to parents in fulfillment of the fourth commandment, and to establishing a Christian peer group for youth to stand strong against the attack. It is a major challenge taken on by many united Christian communities that have declared to Satan, "Enough is enough. You will no longer steal away our children. They belong to the Lord!"

In the past several years, a number of successful youth centered ministries have sprung up. The results are encouraging. The N.E.T. (National Evangelization Team) in Minnesota has gained national acceptance for their work with conferences, retreats and peer witness. The "Life Teen" program of Fr. Dale Fushek and Fr. Jack Spaulding, and the apostolate of Fr. Ken Roberts with youth are two additional examples, and have reached thousands of young people. There are many others.

The fruits of these programs are evident in the lives of the youth involved: a realistic outlook to life and the world, new values and priorities, a recognition of, and need for, Jesus as a Saviour.

There is nothing more important than youth, for therein lies the future of the world.

CHAPTER 11

THE WAR AGAINST
UNITED COMMUNITIES

*Our battle is not against human forces but against
the principalities and powers, the rulers of this world
of darkness, the evil spirits in regions above. You
must put on the armor of God if you are to resist
on the evil day; do all that your duty requires, and
hold your ground. (Eph. 6:12-13).*

In this chapter I want to consider *united* communities, with
the focus on *united.* Certainly the Church, the full community, is continually being attacked in its unity. In the next
chapter we will consider the attacks of Satan against the
Church proper, but here I want to focus in on the lay,
covenanted communities that have really sought to be strongly
united in the Lord, united in one heart and one mind. The
examples I'll be using I am personally acquainted with or
have been involved with. Some of the details I will not bring
out in order to protect the people involved. Other details and
interpretations are described from my point of view, so I ask
forgiveness from any party that I may slight or accidently
misinterpret.

If you want to experience the reality of Satan and his forces,
and see his manifestations, then look to the attacks against
any community strongly and clearly united in a common commitment to the Lord Jesus and to one another. Satan seems
to relish attacking communities that make a commitment to
be of one heart and one mind in the Lord—seeking unity
between themselves, and seeking unity between the divided

churches. His apparent strategy here is to divide and conquer by attacks on the communities in the most blatant way.

The examples of the attacks shown here can be described by one or more, or even all of the following strong words: vicious, virulent, vitriolic, vile, venomous and violent!

• When the ecumenical covenant community, *Word of God*, based in Ann Arbor, Michigan, was first forming in the early 1970's, I was confronted with a number of accusations and harsh judgments against the community before, during and after my two years of living with them. These attacks came largely from women who were members of religious communities, or past members. "Why are they going back to old rigid ways? They are mistreating women! They are fundamentalistic! They are harsh and judgmental." My response was usually, "Why are you so threatened by something that does not concern you? Can they live a committed lifestyle of their choice?"

• When the *Word of God* and *The People of Praise,* a lay covenant community based in South Bend, tried to take steps toward a fuller and deeper common commitment to unity between themselves and a number of associated communities, a rift developed between them over the nature of their style of community life and philosophy, and it was aggravated by differences between strong personalities. Both parties sought sincerely to be in the Lord and in the heart of the Church, and yet a division resulted (shades of Paul and Barnabas). (*See Acts* 15:36-41). But the work of Satan is there in the continued lack of uniting and communication, a division that continues to hinder the renewal.

• *The Bread of Life Community,* based in Akron, Ohio, came under public attack in the mass media (1984-85), for being a cult. A jounalist took it upon himself as an exercise of the "cult watchers" to create an exposé according to his own criteria, wearing his own colored glasses. The attacks can be described by several of the strong "V" words listed earlier! The local ordinary and his auxiliary bishop became involved since the Bread of Life Community had asked for recognition as a community by the local diocese. A more than thorough examination was carried out, but unfortunately it stressed the criteria of current secularized psychology, sociology and management dynamics. Thanks be to God for the humble, loyal obedience of their leaders, which has been able to win the victory.

• *St. Alphonsus Parish* in Langdon, North Dakota, and its pastor and his associate underwent all six of the strong "V" words listed above during 1984. When the spiritual renewal of the parish was "brought up the main aisle," as the pastor described the open and clear focus on renewing the parish, a small clique of reactionaries went to the mass media, and even threatened the pastor with violence. The local police made the pastor wear a bullet-proof vest! The bishop, the late Justin Driscoll, defended the pastor and came to the parish to call for obedience and threatened excommunication against those who were perpetrating the attacks. In the midst of this, the Bishop died of a heart attack. The current Bishop, James Sullivan, understands and supports the pastor, as do the vast majority of the parishioners. But the tensions have not been fully resolved.

• *The People of Hope Community,* based in Berkeley Heights, New Jersey experienced strong attack from local groups. The attacks reached the mass media and carried all the earmarks and stench of Satan's work. Since the community had requested diocesan recognition, the Archbishop initiated an investigation of the community. Again, the methodology and criteria of the investigation, being extensively influenced by secularized psychology, sociology and anthropology, resulted in the request for fundamental changes in their lifestyle and commitment.

The basis of the attacks had to do with the "threat" of the members of the community moving into the Berkeley Heights area and forming a geographic community with their own school.

The question that keeps requesting an answer— "Why does a united community pose such a threat to people?" Why are they so afraid of people who are united in their commitment to live the Gospel as fully as they can? The answer lies in fear and conviction against their own lifestyle. It is all aggravated by the work of Satan and his minions.

And Is There a Solution?

I would suggest two types of defenses, one—"holiness," and the other, "Catholic Doctrine" as fundamental requirements.

"Holiness" is the direct antidote to the vile attacks of Satan. In this case, the holiness needed is first the presence of the Holy Spirit, and then truth, mercy and humility. Without truth, mercy and humility, the Holy Spirit cannot be present. And if the Holy Spirit is not present and working, then other spirits are! Then there are lies, lack of forgiveness, and pride.

"Catholicity" is the combination of the elements of the Catholic Church, that characterizes it as Catholic, namely the Eucharist, Mary, and the Pope and bishops in union with Him. *(See Reference 19)*. If one or more of these elements are missing in a community, then the attacks are all the more destructive. On the other hand, where the local bishop is supportive, and the community is centered on the Eucharist, with a public devotion to Mary, it can withstand the most virulent attacks—even attacks that could be described with all six of the strong "V" words. The parish of St. Alphonsus in Langdon is a case in point.

When a united community experiences the presence of evil forces, it should rejoice! It is hitting Satan where it hurts. So we on earth should follow suit to what has already happened in Heaven:

They defeated him (Satan) *by the blood of the Lamb and by the word of their testimony; love for life did not deter them from death. So rejoice, you heavens and you that dwell therein! But woe to you, earth and sea, for the devil has come upon you! His fury knows no limits, for he knows his time is short.* (Rev. 12:11-12).

It is also interesting to note, that the many claimed apparitions of Our Lady, currently taking place all over the world, are producing great fruits in this type of faith commitment. Prayer groups, and new lay communities are springing up worldwide. They give evidence of strong conversion and renewal, and, not surprisingly, are based on two elements. First, a desire for holiness, and secondly, solid in Church doctrine.

Chapter 12

SATAN AGAINST THE CHURCH PROPER

All the signs point to a Church whose walls of defense are broken down, whose unit is disrupted, and whose structural faults are exposed.

Therefore, I believe it is clear that the Church is in time of travail (*See Rev.* 12), a time of shaking (*See Heb.* 12:28), a time of pruning clean that will increase fruitfulness (*See Jn.* 15:2), a time of trial that will lead to a time of praise (*See 1 Ptr.* 1:7), a time of travail that will lead to joy. (*See Jn.* 16:21).

Pope John XXIII in convoking the Second Vatican Council spoke of "painful considerations":

"Today the Church is witnessing a crisis underway with society. While humanity is on the edge of a new era, tasks of immense gravity and amplitude await the Church, as in the most tragic periods of its history. It is a question, in fact, of bringing the modern world into contact with the vivifying and perennial energies of the Gospel, a world which exalts itself with its conquests in the technical and scientific fields, but which brings also the consequences of a temporal order which some have wished to reorganize excluding God...and hence there is a completely new and disconcerting fact: the existence of a militant atheism which is active on a world level."

Pope John then concluded his convocation with an exhortation to the whole Church to continue in serious prayer. He prayed:

> "Divine Spirit. . .renew Your wonders in this our age as in a new Pentecost, and grant that Your Church, praying perseveringly and insistently with one heart and mind together with Mary, the Mother of Jesus, and guided by blessed Peter, may increase the reign of the Divine Saviour, a reign of truth and justice, a reign of love and peace."

Pope Paul VI, in his encyclical *Paths of the Church,* (See Reference 12) graphically described the attack on the Church by the great transformations, upheavel, and developments which are profoundly changing exterior modes of life, and the very ways of thinking of our times:

> "All of this, like waves of an ocean, envelopes and agitates the Church itself. Men committed to the Church are greatly influenced by the climate of the world; so much so that a danger bordering almost on vertiginous confusion and bewilderment can shake the Church's very foundations and lead mankind to embrace most bizarre ways of thinking, as though the Church should disavow herself and take up the very latest and untried ways of life." (#29).

The situation within the Church was of great concern to the late Pope Paul VI. Throughout the time of his pontification he expressed his concerns in vivid terms. He was keenly aware of destructive criticism and a "polarization of dissent" causing disunity within the Church. *(See Reference 13)*.

In a startling statement, Pope John Paul II, then Karol Cardinal Wojtyla, in his last speech in the United States in September, 1976, as quoted in the New York City News (an interim strike newspaper) described the crisis in the Church and the world in this way:

> "We are now standing in the face of the greatest historical confrontation humanity has gone through.

I do not think that wide circles of the American society, or wide circles of the Christian community, realize this fully. We are now facing the final confrontation between the Church and the anti-Church, of the Gospel versus the anti-Gospel. This confrontation lies within the plans of divine Providence; it is a trial which the whole Church, and the Polish Church in particular, must take up.

"It is a trial of not only our nation and the Church, but in a sense, a test of 2,000 years of culture and Christian civilization with all of its consequences for human dignity, individual rights, human rights and the rights of nations."

Pope John Paul II has begun to lift a corner of the veil that has been hiding a de facto apostasy. His letter to Priests (April 9, 1979), his condemnation of the teachings of a certain theologian and a bishop, plus his other statements in various addresses are drawing a strong and critical reaction on the part of some writers.

It is worthwhile to state the obvious here. Pope John Paul II is not causing the apostasy. He is just revealing in clear light, what is already there, and deep in our hearts, we all know it.

There is more light and unveiling yet to come: Dissent, scandals and divisions. This action and reaction within the Church can be another source of the shaking of the Church, a testing to find out what is made of solid material and what is of straw. (*See 1 Cor.* 3:11-15).

Certain signs of weakness and disunity within the Church stand out clearly:

A polarizing dissent against the very fact of authority, especially against the Magisterium of the Church;

a lack of reverence for the teachings of the Holy Father;

a readiness to follow certain theologians who are in open dissent with the Holy Father and the Magisterium;

an unwillingness to conceive that there could even
be such a thing as submission of heart and mind
in the light of faith.

There is confusion in the teachings in some schools of theology in regard to the very divinity of Christ, His bodily resurrection, the presence of the Lord in the Blessed Sacrament,
the place of Mary in the plan of salvation, and confusion
in moral teachings, especially in the area of sexuality and
the sacredness of life.

The great attack of Satan against the Church is in full
force. The Church, as a united community, has been the
object of vicious and violent attacks from within and from
without in the past that have divided the Church with schisms
and heresies. East and West divided over primacy and juris-
diction; the East splintered over more juridical questions
and dogma, the West fractured by the reformation. Satan
seems to delight in the strategy of "divide and conquer."
What was stated in the chapter on "Satan's Attacks Against
United Communities," certainly applies all the more to a
united Church. The history of the virulent, vitrolic, and
violent attacks has the pugent, sulfurous, stench of Hell
itself—wars, riots, torture, killings, polemics, hatred, anger,
suspicion and bitterness. We have much to repent of, and
much reparation to do—because we are sinners and we have
been duped by Satan.

There is another way to evaluate developments in the Church
today, and that is to take a look at what ought to be its
signs of strength.

These are: Conversion, charisma, community, the Sacra-
ments, the spiritual and corporal works of mercy, unity, peace
and love. The Church is firm when it is built on the foundation of Jesus Christ; when each member experiences the Lord
Jesus in a personal and saving way and experiences daily forgiveness; when each member is gifted with some ministry or
gift to build up the Body of Christ; when the members are
committed to the Lord and one another as their highest priority; when the presence of the Holy Spirit overflows in wor-

ship, service of mercy and evangelization; when the Spirit binds us into a unity of peace and love.

To what extent are these signs truly operative in the Church today?

Another evaluation of the strength of the Church is to consider the present situation in regard to the traditional expressions, those of unity and strength among us, namely, the Eucharist, Mary, the Sacred Scriptures, tradition, teaching and the Pope. The strength of the Roman Catholic Church has been in its solidarity in all of these areas; the Eucharist as the apex of the unity of sacramental life; Mary as the queen of the communion of saints; the Sacred Scriptures as the word of God interpreted by the discernment of the whole Church; teachings on doctrine and morals growing out of the living tradition of the Church; and the local parishes in unity with and part of the whole Church under the visible sign of unity, the Pope.

To what extent are these signs present? It is a question that haunts me, and I suspect it is to a great many other people as well.

It is important to understand that this travail is God's work of purification and that these signs of purification will undoubtedly grow more dramatic before things get better. Rather than be scandalized and depressed by what we perceive happening, we need to understand that the mystery of God's plan of death and resurrection is at work.

End-times or New Travail? "Yes!" and "No!"

No, it is not the end of the world, though it may be the preparation for the Second Coming of the Lord. The Second Coming of the Lord does not mean the end of the world. I believe it means rather that He is coming again to rule the world as the King of Glory. Both the time and manner are the Father's secret. But, yes these are the "end-times" insofar as they are the end of an age as we have known it. The words of the Gospel, of Our Lady speaking in our times, of popes, of prophets, and of analysts of the conditions in the Church and world, all speak of the crisis that is upon us.

The Church is in travail. We can all see its symptoms in the confusion, insubordination, dissent, and even persecution that is part of the Church's life today in many cultures and places in the world. I think that these signs deserve to be taken seriously and to receive the thoughtful and prayerful consideration of all Christians. The response, as at any time in Christian history, is a right relationship with the Lord and with our brothers and sisters. It demands study, prayer and effort, not the naive responses represented by ignoring the issues, shrinking in ignorant fear, or hiding from the signs of the times. *(See Reference 14).*

CHAPTER 13

THE BATTLEFIELD OF THE MIND

A major battlefield in all spiritual warfare is the mind. The father of lies confuses the mind such that the person makes decisions that he would not otherwise make. God created us with freedom. We can freely choose to follow Him and His commandments, or we can choose not to. In a word, we can *sin*. We have a choice, and we are responsible for that choice. This freedom of choice is a precious gift of God, and not even God will violate it. Because of this gift, God has placed Himself in a dilemma, so to speak. On the one hand, He has created us free, and on the other hand, He is in love with us and would love to possess us, but that would violate our freedom. So He hovers over us like a frustrated lover, waiting for us to say "yes" freely, so that He may show us His infinite love. This gift of freedom has been very costly to God, because in creating us with this freedom of choice, He took the terrible risk of our saying "no." And we did just that, collectively in Adam and Eve, and individually by our personal sins. Sin caused the passion and death of the Son of God! What a precious gift this freedom must be!

This freedom of choice, this free will of ours, is the strongest faculty we have, because it is the decision maker. The will is, in its turn, influenced and formed by the mind, emotions and appetites, and makes its decisions according to the information provided by them.

The spiritual warfare, then, is over our wills. Our will is attacked, not directly which would violate our freedom, but rather indirectly using our minds, emotions and appetites.

Evil spirits cannot violate our will, but they can attack our minds and appetites, and so, achieve the same result. If Satan can confuse our minds with lies and doubts, he has confused the data by which we make a decision. So we can begin to grasp the importance of protecting the mind with truth.

We can see how the serpent confused the mind of Adam and Eve with a question of doubt, and thus opened up their appetites and desires against the command of God.

> *The serpent asked the woman, 'Did God really tell you not to eat from any of the trees in the garden?' The woman answered the serpent: 'We may eat of the fruit of the trees in the garden; it is only about the fruit of the tree in the middle of the garden that God said, "you shall not eat it or even touch it, lest you die!" But the serpent said to the woman: 'You certainly will not die! No, God knows that the moment you eat of it your eyes will be opened and you will be like gods who know what is good and what is bad.' The woman saw that the tree was good for food, pleasing to the eyes and desirable for gaining wisdom. So she took some of its fruit and ate it; and she also gave some to her husband, who was with her, and he ate it.* (Gen. 3:1, 7).

Here is the battlefield of the mind. Satan casts doubt. His lies come as something "good," not "evil," lies of being "like gods" with the truth of knowing evil. He confused their minds; their appetites were activated by what appeared to be good, and they made a very bad decision. They ate the fruit of the tree in the middle of the garden in direct disobedience to the command of God. Satan won the battle over their free wills by attacking their minds. Adam and Eve allowed God's truth to be replaced by questioning doubts and lies.

It is precisely over the truth that the battle continues to rage, and the temptations still come to us looking like "good" on the surface, never as obvious "evil." It is the truth that will set us free: *If you will live according to my teaching, you are truly my disciples; then you will know the truth, and the truth will set you free.* (Jn. 8:31-32).

So it is that in many passages of Scripture we are taught the important role of truth in guarding our minds and in transforming our minds into the mind of Christ. Here are a few excerpts:

> *Do not conform yourselves to this age but be transformed by the renewal of your mind.* (*Rom.* 12:2).
> *...acquire a fresh, spiritual way of thinking.* (*Eph.* 4:23-24).
> *We demolish sophistries and every proud pretension that raises itself against the knowledge of God; we likewise bring every thought into captivity to make it obedient to Christ.* (*2 Cor.* 10:4-5).
> *Then God's own peace, which is beyond all understanding, will stand guard over your hearts and minds, in Christ Jesus.* (*Phil.* 4:7).

St. Paul, in forming his disciple Timothy, was deeply concerned about truth and the mind, so he repeatedly urged that sound teaching be given:

> *I charge you to preach the word, to stay with this task whether convenient or inconvenient— correcting, reproving, appealing—constantly teaching and never losing patience. For time will come when people will not tolerate sound doctrine, but following their own desires, will surround themselves with teachers who tickle their ears.* (*2 Tim.* 4:2-4).

Truth is the cornerstone of the battle over the mind. Jesus taught truth and reveals Himself as the Truth because He knew the importance of truth to keep us free.

Over the centuries, the Church has been deeply concerned about truth, knowing full well that without the truth of Jesus Christ and His Gospel, our freedom is destroyed. So the Church has taught through creeds, through councils, through the development of theology, protecting us against false teaching and heresy. The teaching authority of the Church has always been a major part of the pastoral concern for the people of God. Over the ages we have been blessed by the work of doctors of the Church, ministers, theologians and teachers; we have had books and catechisms; we have had extensive training of priests and religious—all this to protect the truth of the Gospel.

The truth will set us free! Again, as stated by John, (See 8:31-32): *If you live according to my teaching, you are truly my disciples; then you will know the truth and the truth will set you free.*

Sometime ago, I wrote an article originally published in "New Covenant" magazine. I quote from it here because it describes in a graphic way the attack of Satan on our mind, and the way to resist the attack!

"What we think affects the way we speak, act, and feel—and even the way we look! Our thoughts affect our whole being.

"Our thoughts are like cassette tapes. We have a whole library of these tapes that can be played at any time. Many of them we have inherited from our culture, and others from Adam and Eve. Our own life experiences contribute to the collection. We record the good, the bad, the joys, and the hurts, to play back at any time. We can play one tape over and over again—perhaps a hurtful situation that we rehearse in our minds, wishfully thinking of how things might have gone better. This kind of tape cassette affects our whole being.

"We know the Christian response to tapes that drag us down: Push the eject button! We do not have to play the old tapes over and over again. We can replace our library of old tapes with new ones that build us up instead.

"By 'thoughts' I mean all that goes on in our heads— reflections, reasonings, calculations, planning, judgments, evaluations, imaginings, and daydreaming. Some thoughts are good, constructive, creative, and upbuilding. Other thoughts are not so good: they breed contempt, confusion, hatred, lust, division, and all sorts of evil.

"The connection between our thoughts and the reaction of our body, mind, and spirit is very real. For example, we have been taught and we know from experience the effect of lustful thoughts and how they can lead to lustful action. Similarly, judgmental thoughts lead to judgment, resentful thoughts to hatred, jealous thoughts to division. The list can go on and on. The point is that unguarded thoughts can direct the whole person.

"It is also true, however, that instead of continually replaying negative thoughts we can erase them like a tape cassette and replace them with thoughts and memories that build on faith. Healing of the hurtful memories by prayer is an effective way to erase those tapes.

"Paul puts it this way: *Dismiss all anxiety from your minds.* (*Phil.* 4:6). Get rid of the old tapes! Then he tells us to play another set of tapes: *Finally, my brothers, your thoughts should be wholly directed to all that is true, all that deserves respect, all that is honest, pure, admirable, decent, virtuous, or worthy of praise. ...Then the God of peace will be with you.* (*Phil.* 4:8-9).

"Paul is very aware that our thoughts are connected to actions. Whatever thought that is not of Christ, Paul dismisses.

"With Paul we can ask each thought for its visa and passport: 'Where are you from? What are you doing here?' If from the evil one or his spirits, we can order the thought to be gone. If from our own spirit or from our own past. We can eject it—like an old cassette—and put in a new one.

"This is what it means to guard our thoughts in Christ Jesus. Thoughts of rejoicing in the Lord, giving thanks, thoughts of compassion and mercy, are of the Lord Jesus. These are the ones we should play over and over again, maybe even turning up the volume!

"This is the point of Jesus' parable on the good and bad tree. He told the Pharisees, *How can you utter anything good, you brood of vipers, when you are so evil? The mouth speaks whatever fills the mind. A good man produces good from his store of goodness; and evil man produces evil from his evil store.* (*Matt.* 12:34-35).

"This is also Jesus' teaching on what makes us impure: *It is not what goes into a man's mouth that makes him impure; it is what comes out of his mouth. ... Do you not see that everything that enters the mouth passes into the stomach and is discharged into the latrine, but what comes out of the mouth originates in the mind? It is things like these that make a man impure. From the mind stems evil designs—murder, adulterous conduct, fornication, stealing, false witness, blasphemy. These are the things that make a man impure. As for eating with unwashed hands that makes no man impure.* (Matt. 15:11, 15-20).

"Ignatius Loyola discovered for himself the importance of guarding his thoughts. While in the hospital recuperating from a leg wound, Ignatius spent his time reading novels about romantic heroes. He was delighted with his favorite pastime. But when he had no more novels to read he began reading the lives of saints, also with great delight.

"Soon, however, Ignatius noticed a major difference. After he had been reading the lives of heroes his thoughts became morbid and depressed, but after reading the lives of the saints his thoughts continued to be uplifted. This was the insight that led Ignatius to develop his method of discernment. He taught his disciples to check out the origin of thoughts and the pattern that followed afterwards.

"Our thoughts really do affect our patterns of feeling and behavior. It is worthwhile to check out the origins of our thoughts. Do they come from some old cassette we let play over and over again? Do they come from our unguarded reading, our unguarded viewing of television, our unguarded conversations, or our unguarded eyes?

"Our real freedom of mind will come from our relationship with Christ Jesus. Whatever thought is not of Christ— that is, any thought that does not build my faith in Jesus and my love for His church—should be recognized as such. We should ask its origin and purpose, ask for its passport. If it is not of Christ, then we reject it and ask Christ to stand guard over our hearts and minds with His peace."

CHAPTER 14

THE CHRISTED MAN—
A CHRISTIAN ANTHROPOLOGY

I have come to realize the need of a new way of understanding mankind in order to emphasize what God wants to do in our lives in the midst of spiritual warfare. I was taught to consider man as a rational animal, two-dimensional. The rationality of man was the unique trait that set him apart from a wide variety of animals, a prime factor in determining his actions and goals (both genders intended).

But there is a difficulty with this emphasis on the intellect, because our primary relationship with God is not intellectual. We are not able to grasp the mystery of God within our intellect. Our relationship with God, however, is not opposed to reason; rather it is beyond reason; and if we insist on understanding the mystery of God before accepting it, then we cut ourselves off from a whole dimension of reality.

There is a third dimension in mankind, the spirit; the touch of God within us that longs for communion with God. It is as much a dimension of the whole person as the dimensions of rationality and animality. The spirituality of a person is not a part that can be divided from the whole. If I consider myself to be just a rational animal, I eliminate the whole dimension of life-power, of intuition, of creative communion, and I limit myself to what I can touch, what I can understand with my mind, and what I can control. The human spirit is so delicate that it can be limited and even suppressed by the dominance of rationality or animality.

Scripture and tradition have accepted the human spirit as

real. So it is important for us to re-evaluate this dimension of our being because it is through this dimension that the Holy Spirit of the Father and Son touches and enters our being. This is the touch-point of God and mankind. *When we cry, 'Abba, Father!' it is the Spirit himself bearing witness with our spirit that we are children of God.* (Rom. 8:15-16).

Our Human Spirit

Our human spirit is the touch point of God's Spirit. Usually, God does not touch our minds, wills and bodies directly but rather touches us through our human spirit. We need to understand who we are and who God is if we are to cooperate with Him. We need to understand the Holy Spirit as the *Gift* of the Father touching our spirit. We also need to understand ourselves as made in the image of the Trinity.

To some people, the mention of spirit conjures up thoughts and impressions of the magical. This should not be. The area of the spiritual is now beginning to be rediscovered, even as the areas of our psychological and bodily makeup have been clarified in the past.

Our bodily functions were, at one time, considered to be magical until anatomical and physiological investigations showed them to be real. So, too, the areas of our subconscious and functions of the psychological were considered a dark void until the advance of the studies of psychology. Now, in our times, the investigation of events beyond the psychological are being brought into the light.

Such events as extrasensory perception, luminescence, healing do exist. Man has extraordinary powers unknown to himself. They may be suppressed by fear or superstition, ignorance, or by the dominance of the intellect. They can also lead us in the wrong direction through over-zealous beliefs in our own power, as seen in the "New Age" practices of today.

The human spirit is oriented toward communion with other spirits and moved by them. For this reason the discernment of spirits is the key gift needed in dealing with movements of the spirit. It is essential to discern what spirit is moving my spirit. Is it a human spirit (mine or another human being), an angelic spirit (good or evil) or is it the Holy Spirit? As

Christians we are called to be open to the Holy Spirit and his promptings and no other. So for a Christian to be experimenting with his own human spirit by opening himself up to unknown spirits is not only dangerous but idolatrous.

A Biblical Anthropology of Man

Sacred Scripture reveals the nature of the human as well as the nature of God. It would be good to recognize that God has something to say about the way He made us. The most fundamental picture of mankind is that we are created by God as one whole being. We are a unity, however, that can be looked at from different points of view. We are a unity of body-soul-spirit, not divided into three parts, but rather one person related to all things around us. We are in relationship. As *body* or "flesh," we are related to all things that are created, sharing with them the commonness of creaturehood. As *soul*, we are unique and yet related to living things. As *spirit,* we are oriented to or related to God, Who is Spirit, communing with Him.

In Hebrew, there are three words for person: *bashar,* meaning body-person; *nephesh*, meaning soul-person; and *ruah,* meaning a spirit-person. The phrase "I am body, or I am soul, or I am spirit" is closer to Hebrew thought than "I have a body, I have a soul, or I have a spirit." The Hebrews used the terms: *bashar, nephesh, ruah,* to describe the whole man in three different relationships.

In keeping with the Hebraic love of earthly descriptions, man might also be described in the English terms, heart, head and hand. Heart suggests the inner person that longs for God (spirit). Head refers to the unique, living, thinking person (soul), and hand denotes the helping and working person, the strength of man (body). In this sense, the Great Commandment of Deuteronomy 6:5 can be understood as loving God with the totality of our being. *You shall love the Lord, your God, with all your heart, and all your soul, and all your strength.*

Other Descriptions of Man

St. Paul uses the three-fold description of man as spirit-soul-body only once in *1 Thess.* 5:23. His most common anthropology, however, is man as spirit and flesh (sarx) where the flesh is used in the sense of the unredeemed man, and the spirit as the spiritual man. But generally in the scripture (and occasionally in Paul's writings), the word *sarx* (flesh, body) has a two-fold meaning; man as created matter (good), or man as unredeemed (sinful). St. Paul uses another word *soma* for body, with several meanings: our created body which is the temple of the Holy Spirit, the assembly of the people of God (Church), and the eucharistic body of Christ. The important thing to realize is that whatever term he uses, he describes the whole person.

St. Thomas Acquinas uses the anthropology of body and soul. In his use of the term "soul," the functions of the spirit include intuition and conscience. There is a definite need to make explicit the two dimensions of the soul to see clearly the role of the human spirit, the inner man, communing with the Holy Spirit. The delicate separation of the spirit from the soul is described in the words of the Letter to the Hebrews:

> *For the word of God is living and active, sharper than any two-edged sword, piercing to the division of soul and spirit, of joints and marrow, and discerning the thoughts and intentions of the heart.*
> (*Heb.* 4:12).

Man is a Spiritual Being

When the Eastern Fathers stress in their spirituality that we are a spiritual being, they are stressing that our spirit, not our rationality, is to be queen of our being. The point of emphasis is on the dominance of the spirit, not on the elimination of reason. This means that the spiritual life is one where our human spirit is open to the presence and prompting of the Holy Spirit, and that we live in communion with God.

They further stress the fact that we are made in the image and likeness of God and this image and likeness must also be Trinitarian. It is the Holy Spirit that unites our being and makes it a new creation. This stress on the spirit avoids the Pelagian tendencies of the Western Church, that is, the implication that I reach holiness by my efforts, rather than by accepting a gift.

In our western tradition, we have placed our rationality as the queen of our being. When someone says "you are logical," or "you are using your reason," we automatically take it as a compliment. But is such a remark always a compliment? It assumes that the greatest thing that I can do is be rational or logical. Wouldn't it be more of a compliment to say you are "spiritual?"

Of course we can go to the opposite extreme of not using our reason. This is no solution to the difficulty. The intellect is a servant of the whole person. Its role is to test, analyze, synthesize, compare, to abstract and essentialize. But its role is not one of setting the ultimate goals in such a way that everything must be understood or controlled before it is accepted by faith in God.

The dominance of the rational in ourselves can be a hindrance to the simple faith that is so needed to live the life in the Spirit. If I insist that I understand and control everything before I accept it into my life, I limit my capacity. The full potential of our vocation as Christians is realized as we allow the Holy Spirit to take control of our lives.

Three Dimension Balance

To be a whole person all three dimensions, spirit, soul and body, need to be operative. A neglect of one dimension to the detriment of the others results in a terrible imbalance.

We cannot neglect our rationality, avoiding all study and teaching, because this would be to misuse this gift. Nor can we neglect our body avoiding proper diet, exercise and rest, without doing harm to ourself. There seems to be a tendency in us to move toward one of the extreme dimensions, to the neglect of the other. For example, some people will experience a deep renewal of the spirit and then depend solely on the gifts of the Spirit to guide their lives, with no study or submission to teachers. Or some will depend solely on spiritual healing, not making use of the gifts God has given a medical doctor when sickness comes upon them. For the correct balance of the three dimensions, all the laws of the body, soul, and spirit must be understood.

When we act, the whole person is involved with one, two or three dimensions. Emotions are an expression of the whole person involving the soul and body. They are tools in aiding us to live and communicate. Emotions are used to express our inner feelings, not to govern our inner feelings. For example, we use anger to express strong feelings, but we cannot let anger use us by lingering on as resentment. Jesus used anger, but did not let anger possess Him. We can express joy in laughter, but not let laughter possess us. Emotions need expression. In our times we do not know how to use them; rather they use us.

The Christian event adds a whole new dimension. God sent His Son to dwell among us and thus inserted Himself into the history of humanity. And more than that, God has sent the Spirit of His Son to dwell within us. We have been given a new spirit, the Holy Spirit, making us truly free, truly whole, and truly holy by penetrating our whole being. As Jesus took on our humanity, so now in exchange, He has given us a share in His divinity by giving us His Spirit, making us sons and daughters of God.

Our wholeness means to be wholly possessed and led by the Holy Spirit. It is the Spirit of the Son that truly sets us free to do the works of the Father. It is in the Holy Spirit that we find our fulfillment and completion.

Holiness is total possession and guidance by the Holy Spirit. In the Letter to the Thessalonians, St. Paul describes how holiness comes about:

> *May the God of peace himself sanctify you wholly; and may your spirit and soul and body be kept sound and blameless at the coming of our Lord Jesus Christ. He who calls you is faithful, and he will do it.* (*1 Thess.* 5:23).

Holiness is the work of the Lord. He is the one Who calls us and accomplishes the work of sanctification in us. It is His gift, but we must accept the gift of His Spirit to possess us and work through us. Since this holiness is a gift and not something we merit, we must ask for it.

The Holy Spirit

The very same Spirit by which Jesus was conceived, by which He did the works of the Father, and by which He was raised from the dead, has been offered to each of us. This gift of the Spirit is a free gift offered with love. In no way will God violate our freedom; we must freely ask for and accept the gift of God. As we freely accept the gift of God, the Spirit can do the works of the Father in us. He will do for us the same things that Jesus did for His disciples: He will call us, baptize us, teach us, remind us, be with us, rebuke us, empower us, be a witness of Jesus to us, and be a helping presence in our need.

We are being called to a union with God. He wants to possess us totally: spirit, soul and body. He wants to dwell in us: "He yearns jealously over the spirit which he has made to dwell in us." (*Jas.* 4:5).

This is the Good News. God Who is love, loves us and gives us His own Spirit to dwell in our hearts that we too may cry, "Father!"

There are many obstacles to the total penetration of the Holy Spirit, among them, our free will. We are free to accept the gift of the Holy Spirit, or reject it, for God will not force Himself upon us and so violate our freedom. We must invite Him to come into our whole being—not just once, but continually, that He might dwell in us and overflow to others.

Sin is a major obstacle, especially the sin of resentment. Resentment can arise from a lack of forgiveness toward ourselves or from a lack of forgiveness of others. Resentment sits very deeply within our spirit and deadens it with its lingering attitudes towards parents, or those in authority, or fellow workers. St. Mark records for us the need to forgive; *And whenever you stand praying, forgive, if you have anything against anyone; so that your Father who is in heaven may forgive you your trespasses.* Resentment is a great detour sign, telling the Spirit to turn away.

Lack of faith is also a block to the Spirit. Jesus could not work miracles where there was a lack of faith, an environment that made the flow of the Spirit impossible. The

Lord asks us to have faith in Him. Our rationality is another obstacle. We have a great tendency to limit by our mind—if we don't understand, it cannot be.

The flesh, in the sense of the unredeemed flesh, is also a major obstacle to the freedom of the spirit and to unconditional yielding to the Spirit. As Jesus warned: *Watch and pray that you may not enter into temptation; the spirit is willing but the flesh is weak.* (Mk. 14:38). A life that is centered on the pleasures of the flesh cannot be centered in the Spirit.

The three dimensional picture of man gives an insight into the effect of original sin. The effect was to disturb the delicate position of the human spirit. As a result of the fall, the spirit was no longer the queen of the being. The flesh began to demand its share and so did the reason and will. Disorder within us continues to show up as passion and pride which are expressed in a variety of ways. Our spirit is trapped by our own sin and kept in bondage of the evil one.

The Redemption by Jesus, offered each of us, gives us the opportunity to be restored to a whole person. He has cut us loose from sin and bondage by giving us a new spirit, His own Spirit.

The very nature of our spirit is to be open to other spirits. Its function is to be in communion with other spirits. This openness of the spirit is beautiful, but at the same time dangerous. As we open our spirit, we are vulnerable to other spirits that are not welcome, including the evil spirits. We have been warned of this by masters of spiritual life. As we open ourselves to the Spirit of God in full commitment, the evil one begins a serious attack upon us.

Jesus Himself experienced this attack after His baptism in the Jordan. When the Holy Spirit came down upon Him, He was led into the desert to be tempted by the devil. Jesus warned the disciples to watch and pray that they be not put to the test. St. James said: *Submit yourselves therefore to God. Resist the devil and he will flee from you.* (Jas. 4:7).

St. Peter taught: *Humble yourselves therefore under the mighty hand of God that, in due time, he may exalt you. Cast all your anxieties on him, for he cares about you. Be sober, be watchful. Your adversary, the devil, prowls around like a roaring lion, seeking someone to devour. Resist him, firm in your faith.* (1 Ptr. 5:6-9).

So all spirits must be tested to see that they are of the Lord:

Beloved, do not believe every spirit, but test the spirits to see whether they are of God; for many false prophets have gone into the world. By this you know the Spirit of God: every spirit that confesses that Jesus Christ has come in the flesh is of God, and every spirit which does not confess Jesus is not of God. (1 Jn. 4:1-3).

When we yield to the Holy Spirit, we experience freedom and power to do the works of the Father. This freedom is a mark of the Holy Spirit.

Prayer in the Spirit

Prayer can involve the whole person in such a way that our spirit yields to the Holy Spirit crying out to the Father. Prayer should be a cooperation of our whole being, with the Holy Spirit.

In a sense, prayer is not so much something I do, as much as something I allow to happen in and through me. Prayer is the Spirit of the Living God in me and through Jesus, worshipping the Father. Prayer is my active cooperation with the Spirit primarily through total submission to His presence and action. Prayer is a cooperative venture of the Spirit of Christ Jesus continuing the work of pleasing the Father in and through me. My part is to yield and cooperate with the presence and workings of the Holy Spirit.

Cooperation means effort. Sometimes the effort is a struggle to be faithful and persevering. Sometimes it is a battle against temptation of the evil one who doesn't want us to yield.

Cooperation means that I must use my will and my intelligence to stir up my spirit to abide in a joyful peace.

Cooperation means that we really have been created free to worship and serve the Lord. My free cooperative worship and service does, in fact, add to the glory of the Father. Our greatness is that we have been given the Spirit of the Living God to freely worship and serve the Father.

Jesus has revealed the Father to us and has given us their Holy Spirit that we, too, might please the Father even as Jesus did. Prayer is drawing upon that power promised us.

CHAPTER 15

THE HEALTHY PERSON

It is in prayer that we face the reality of the attacks of sin, the influence of the world around us and the forces of the evil one. It is necessary to pray if we are to drink the healing cup the Father offers us and fend off spiritual attacks. It is in prayer that we encounter ourselves, for we allow the Lord to reach down deep into our inner selves and point out the hidden areas of darkness and sin. It is in prayer that we take the risk of exposing ourselves to the Lord, so that He might heal us to the depths of our inner being. Prayer is a risk, because we expose all that we are, but prayer is also healing, because we expose ourselves to the Divine Physician. It is in prayer that we invite the Lord to accomplish His work of conversion and redemption.

I am coming to understand more fully that because of the spiritual weakness of our defenses, our most vulnerable area is the spiritual. Are not many sicknesses ultimately due to sin? My own personal sin and the overwhelming cumulative sin of all mankind is a force that keeps sickness in the world. If we are to be healed, we also need to repent and confess our sins by turning to the Lord Jesus, Who alone takes away the sins of the world. For total healing, we need the healing power of Jesus Who alone is able to heal us spiritually.

Our spiritual defenses are also communal and so we "pray constantly and attentively for all in the holy company." (*Eph.* 6:19). Through prayer we are supported by the defenses of Christian community. This is what the Church is about; it is a defense against the attacks of the world and the devil.

It is a graced environment in which we can be freely Christian without apologizing for our faith and piety. In an environment of faith, hope and love, we are sustained in spiritual health, mutually protected by the strength of God's power and by the working of the Holy Spirit.

Without Christian community to support us, we are easily overwhelmed. I am coming to the realization that an explicit Christ-centered community, a community of faith, hope and love is essential for full health.

Pneumo-Psycho-somatic Defenses

Our *whole* being reacts and interacts when under attack, because we are one whole being, not divided into parts. If we are spiritually sick, our mind and body are affected, and so also if our body is sick, our spirit and mind suffer with it. A large majority of sicknesses are complicated by the interaction of the *psyche* and *soma*. Psychosomatic sickness is very common and yet very real. The cause may be psychological, but it expresses itself in a biological way. Continued tension in your living situation, for example, can express itself in bleeding ulcers. The ulcers are real—you can die from them—but the origin of the sickness is not biological, but psychological. Your stomach can be operated on to repair the damage, but the ulcers will occur again if the tension is not dealt with.

In a similar way, a sickness may be spiritual in origin and express itself psychologically and biologically. If a man commits murder, either by a gun or by his tongue in ruining someone's reputation, the person will suffer in his whole being. I am coming to understand that all sickness is pneumo-psycho-somatic. That is, all sickness can be traced to a disruption of the defenses of one of these three realms. Further, I would venture to say that much of the sickness we experience has its ultimate cause in the spiritual realm.

Sin is the underlying root of world sickness.

Weakening of any of our defenses opens us up to sickness and weakness at all levels. That is why St. Paul prays that we be whole and entire:

May the God of peace make you perfect in holiness, may he preserve you whole and entire, spirit, soul and body, irreproachable at the coming of our Lord Jesus Christ. He who calls you is trustworthy, therefore he will do it. (*I Thess.* 5:23).

The God of peace wants us to be at peace, i.e. in right order within ourselves, with others, and above all with God Himself. Only the Lord's peace is capable of preserving us whole and entire. This is God's desire; He really wants to make us perfect in holiness and will to do it if we allow Him. To allow God to make us whole and entire, we need to freely ask Him to come into our hearts and do a work of healing. But as a faithful and loving God, He longs with an everlasting love to heal us, to set us at peace, to make us healthy, to make us whole and entire, to make us perfect in holiness.

Communal Health

To be fully healthy, a community must be healthy in all three realms. Biological and psychological health is good, but not sufficient. We need spiritual health as well.

Communities that are total communities, such as religious congregations, need to be continually renewed at these three levels. Spiritual health is of prime importance. Only the community that experiences continual conversion to the Lord will experience lasting vitality. Biological and psychological renewal are important, but these are not the goal of renewal. A healthy community provides an atmosphere of defense against spiritual, psychological, and biological attacks. A renewal or strengthening of only one of these dimensions is not enough because it still leaves us vulnerable.

St. Paul reminds us that we are one body and that we are responsible to preserve the unity among us:

Make every effort to preserve the unity which has the Spirit as its origin and peace as its binding force. There is but one body and one Spirit, just as there is but one hope given all of you by your call. (*Eph.* 4:3-4).

Our relationships with one another, and the Lord, need to be knit together by the Spirit. The Spirit of Jesus among us makes us one. We need to pray for that Spirit and work to preserve it by removing all obstacles to the presence of the Spirit.

Again St. Paul teaches about health of the community in his teaching on the Eucharist. To the community of Corinth which was divided because of factions, he tells them that they must recognize the *body* of the Lord if they are to avoid being sick, infirm, and spiritually dead. The recognition of the body is in two senses: 1. The body of the Lord as His flesh under the sign of bread and 2. The body of the Lord as the assembled people one in His Spirit.

> *A man should examine himself first; only then should he eat of the bread and drink of the cup. He who eats and drinks without recognizing the body eats and drinks a judgment on himself. That is why many among you are sick and infirm, and why so many are dying.* (2 Cor. 11:28-30).

To be a healthy community, we need to recognize that we are one body. We are the body of the Lord. To be healthy, we need to be one in Him.

This is the kingdom of Heaven we pray for and work for daily. This is our goal and cry: "Come, Lord Jesus."

CHAPTER 16

ADVENT! COME, LORD JESUS!

Come, Lord Jesus!

The coming of the Lord Jesus is the triumph of the spiritual person in spiritual warfare. It is only the coming of the Lord that will bring the final resolution. For this reason, the Church continues to cry out in her travail, "Come, Lord Jesus! Maranatha!" Come with fullness of Your kingdom.

I am writing this in the midst of Advent—the time of preparation for the coming of the Lord. Each liturgy of the Eucharist, each liturgy of the Hours, increases its yearning and cry. "Come, Lord Jesus." He is near. Get ready. Be prepared!

The hymn, "O come, O come Emmanuel" is a cry based on the "Antiphons" of the final week before Christmas Day. The third verse is especially appropriate to the topic of these writings:

> "O come, thou Sprout of Jesse's tree
> Free us from Satan's tyranny!
> From fires of hell thy people save,
> And give us victory o'er the grave.
>
> *Refrain:*
>
> Rejoice! Rejoice! O Israel,
> To thee shall come Emmanuel."

The victory will not come until Jesus returns. Satan's hold on the world is broken when mankind accepts the victory of the cross of Jesus Christ. Some hard facts must be considered in this matter of the coming of the Lord. We have too easily interpreted away the fact of His coming, and we live as though it had no reality. We need to accept, in a real way, that **Jesus is coming again. This is a fact of our faith.** We profess it in the Creed at Mass (Nicene Creed), we proclaim it in every Eucharist, and we pray for it in every Our Father— "Thy Kingdom come!"

We need to live as though He were coming immediately and we need to prepare ourselves by watching, waiting and praying. This is the Gospel teaching. When He is coming we do not know—that knowledge is reserved for the Father— but we *do* know that He will come in glory upon the clouds, and we must be ready to greet Him at whatever hour He comes.

St. Bernard describes three comings of the Lord: His coming in Palestine, His final coming to judge the living and the dead, and a third coming which is in between the other two, a coming presently into our hearts. This third or middle coming is invisible while the other two are visible. *(See Appendix)*.

These facts need to be understood and their implication lived out. Also, the signs of the times need to be interpreted in the light of the Gospel of His coming again. The following are some interpretations that have significance for our way of living:

I believe that there is a "fourth" coming of the Lord— coming to rule the world as king of Glory. It is like two stages of the Final coming—a preparation for His final coming in judgment of the living and the dead. In store for the Church is a new life when we will radiate the presence of the Lord. The Church prays in the liturgy (December 17): "as you nourish us with the food of life, give us also your Spirit so that we may be radiant with light at the coming of Christ, your Son, who is Lord forever and ever. Amen."

Here is the way we describe God's plan in *The Spirit and the Bride Say, Come! (See Reference 13)*:

"God is preparing the Church, His bride, by purifying her. (*Cf. Eph.* 5:26). This work is yet to be completed. Completion will be the new Pentecost prayed for by John XXIII. It will bring about the reign of Jesus as Lord in a glorious Church. To complete the Father's plan, Jesus is to return in order to reign with His purified bride, the Church. This coming of Jesus is not His Final coming, but it is His coming in glory to reign in the hearts of the faithful. It will be a reign of resplendence with the light of Christ shining in the hearts of all believers. It will be a renewed Church of Light, a Light that will bring salvation to all the nations."

We may wonder why the Lord is slow in coming but there are clear indications in the Sacred Scriptures that the delay is due to us—not the Lord. The Lord is waiting for us:

> *But Jesus offered one sacrifice for sins and took his seat forever at the right hand of God. Now he waits until his enemies are placed beneath his feet.* (Heb. 10:13).

Christ is waiting for us, through God's power, to do our part in placing His enemies under His feet! And again:

> *Christ must reign* until *God has put all enemies under his feet.* (1 Cor. 15:25).

It is important to realize this word "until" has special meaning as used in Scripture:

> *Every time, then, you eat this bread and drink this cup, you proclaim the death of the Lord* until *he comes!* (1 Cor. 11:26).

According to J. Jeremias in the *Eucharistic Words of Jesus,* (See Reference 17), the word "until" expresses not only "a time when," but also a purpose. For "until," we can substitute "in order that." This means we can hasten the day of the Lord. A devotion of mercy and standing firm against Satan is what the Lord is waiting for. He wants to show His mercy on all since He wants none to perish but all to come to repentance. (See 2 Ptr. 3:9). So the Lord waits, generation after generation, to show His mercy.

The times we live in are a time to turn to the mercy of God. This is the day of mercy before His coming as judge of justice. Now is the time to turn to His mercy so that He might crush the head of Satan, purify us from our sins, and place death itself beneath His feet.

This is the time of a new Advent—a new coming of the

Lord. Pope John Paul II in his first Encyclical, "Redemptor Hominis," and again in his Encyclical, "Dominum et Viviticantem," refers to the year 2,000 as the "new Advent." He asks: "What should we do in order that this new Advent of the Church, connected with the approaching end of the second millenium, may bring us closer to Him whom Sacred Scripture calls *Everlasting Father? (See Reference 10)*. It is certain that the Church of the new Advent, the Church that is continually preparing for the new coming of the Lord, must be the Church of the Eucharist and of Penance. He seems to have a mystic sense about the new Advent and the beginning of the third millenium—that it needs to be a time of Eucharist and mercy!

I think of the third millenium in light of what St. Peter said: *In the Lord's eyes, one day is as a thousand years and a thousand years are as a day.* (2 *Ptr.* 3:8). It would mean that we are but entering the "third day" which is the day of resurrection for the Church now in travail. It would be the coming of the Lord, a day of glory, the day of the glorious reign of the Lord with His purified Church.

Mary, our Mother and our Queen prepares us for the new Advent of the Lord. She is the woman of Revelation, who prepares us for the coming of the Lord.

Mary, as our Lady of Guadalupe, has shown us that she has crushed the stone serpent. Now she wants to imprint her image of victory, not on a mantle of cactus fiber, but on the fibers of our heart. The victory of Christ Jesus is given to the woman, Our Mother who forms us into the image of her Son Jesus.

At Fatima, this woman of victory confirmed the many scriptural passages that show us the practical steps we must take to fulfill our part in the coming of the Lord in His new Advent. We are to keep the commandments and give witness to Jesus by our lives, actions and words; that is, the duties of our state in life. We are to be the offspring of the woman (*See Rev.* 12:17) and accept her as our own by consecration to her. We are to be strong in our faith and fight the good fight. (*See 1 Tim.* 1:19). We have the victory in Christ Jesus; let's enjoy the fight! In a word, sin no more, be vigilant and *pray*, interceding for the victory, especially through the Rosary.

In praying for victory in the spiritual warfare we could pray three basic prayers: Lord have mercy!; Come, Holy Spirit!; Come Lord Jesus!

> *Lord have mercy!* on us and on the whole world. God wants to have mercy on all—but only those who are humble can receive His mercy. So we pray for the receptivity of all of us sinners to God's infinite mercy.

> *Come, Holy Spirit!*—only the Holy Spirit can heal our wounds in this battle and make us one. Only the Holy Spirit can heal the deep wounds of a divided Church and world.

> *Come, Lord Jesus!*—only the new Advent of the Lord Jesus can bring the final resolution and victory in this spiritual warfare. Only the kingdom of God can give us peace and justice. So with the whole Church, we cry in every Eucharist: "Our Father, who art in heaven, hallowed by Thy name;

> *"Thy kingdom come;* Thy will be done on earth as it is in heaven. Give us this day our daily bread; and forgive us our trespasses as we forgive those who trespass against us; and lead us not into temptation, but *deliver us from evil* (the Evil one). Deliver us, Lord, from every evil, and grant us peace in our day. In your mercy keep us free from sin and protect us from all anxiety as we wait in joyful hope for the coming of our Saviour, Jesus Christ. For the kingdom, the power and the glory are yours, now and forever." **Come, Lord Jesus!**

REFERENCES

1. *Deliver Us From Evil,* general audience of Pope Paul VI, November 15, 1972, *(see the text in Appendix A).*

2. *Pope Paul VI, Prophet of our time, in memoriam, Review for Religious,* 37, 1978, G. W. Kosicki.

3. The Second Vatican Council, *Dogmatic Constitution on the Church (Lumen Gentium).*

4. The Second Vatican Council. *The Pastoral* Constitution on the Church in the Modern World *(Gaudium et Spes).*

5. *Rich in Mercy (Dives in Misericordia),* the second encyclical letter of Pope John Paul II, 1980.

6. *Redeemer of Man (Redemptor Hominis),* the first encyclical letter of Pope John Paul II, 1979.

7. *The Ratzinger Report: an Exclusive Interview on the State of the Church,* Joseph Cardinal Ratzinger with Vittorio Messori, translated by Salvator Attenasio and Graham Harrison, Ignatius Press, San Francisco, 1985.

8. *Humanae Vitae,* encyclical letter of Pope Paul VI, 1968.

9. *Christian Faith and Demonology,* The Sacred Congregation for the Doctrine of the Faith, June 26, 1975.

10. *On Being a Catholic Christian,* G. W. Kosicki, *Review for Religious,* 1982.

11. *Humanae Salutis,* Pope John XXIII's convocation of the Second Vatican Council, December 25, 1961.

116   *Spiritual Warfare*

12. *Pathways of the Church* (Ecclesiam Suam), encyclical letter of Pope Paul VI, 1964.

13. *Paterna Cum Benevelenta,* Pope Paul VI, 1974.

14. Adapted from the book *Pilgrimage and Purification: The Church in Travail in the 80's,* G. W. Kosicki, Crux, Clarity Publishing, Albany, N.Y. 12204, 1980.

15. *The Spirit and the Bride say, Come!* G. Farrell, M.M., and G. W. Kosicki, C.S.B., Ave Maria Institute Press, Asbury, N.J., 08802, 1981.

16. *Born of Mary,* G. W. Kosicki, C.S.B., Marian Press, Stockbridge, MA, 01262, 1986.

17. *The Eucharistic Words of Jesus,* SCM Press, London, 1966, p 253.

DELIVER US FROM EVIL

During the General Audience on November 15, 1972, Paul VI delivered the following address.

What are the greatest needs of the Church today? Do not let our answer surprise you as being over-simple or even superstitious and unreal: one of the greatest needs is defense from that evil which is called the Devil.

Before clarifying our thought, we invite you to open up to the light of faith on the view of human life, a view which from this observation post sweeps over immense distances and penetrates to extraordinary depths. The picture we are invited to contemplate with overall realism is really very beautiful. It is the picture of creation, the work of God, which God Himself admired in its substantial beauty, as the exterior mirror of His wisdom and of His power. *(Cf. Gen. 1:10 etc.)*.

Very interesting, too, is the picture of the dramatic history of humanity, from which there emerges the history of redemption, that of Christ, of our salvation, with its wonderful treasures of revelation, prophecy, holiness, life raised to a supernatural level, eternal promises *(Cf. Eph. 1:10)*. If we look at this picture in the right way, we cannot but remain enchanted *(Cf. St. Augustine, Soliloquies)*: everything has a meaning, everything has a purpose, everything has an order, and everything gives us a glimpse of a Transcendency-Presence, a Thought, a Life, and finally a Love, so that the universe, by what it is and what it is not, presents itself to us as an exalting and elating preparation for something even more beautiful and even more perfect *(Cf. 1 Cor. 2:9; 13:12; Rom. 19-23)*. The

Christian view of the cosmos and life is therefore triumphantly optimistic; and this view justifies our joy and our thankfulness in living, so that celebrating the glory of God we sing of our happiness. *(Cf. the "Gloria" of the Mass)*.

The Teaching of the Bible

But is this view complete? Is it exact? Do we not care anything about the deficiencies in the world? The ways in which things go wrong as regards our existence? Pain, death, wickedness, cruelty, sin, in a word, evil? Do we not see how much evil there is in the world? Particularly, how much moral evil, simultaneously, though in different ways, against man and against God? Is this not a sorry spectacle, an inexplicable mystery? Is it not we followers of the Word, singers of the Good, we believers, who are most sensitive, most upset by the observation and experience of evil?

We find it in the kingdom of nature, where so many of its manifestations seem to us to indicate a disorder. Then we find it among men, where we meet with weakness, frailty, pain, death, and something worse; a dual conflicting law, one desiring good, the other directed to evil, a torment that St. Paul highlights with humiliating clarity to show the necessity and the good fortune of a saving grace, that is, the salvation brought by Christ *(Cf. Rom. 7)*. The pagan poet had already spoken of this inner conflict in man's own heart: "video meliora proboque, deteriora sequor." (Ovid. *Met.* 7:19). We find sin, the perversion of human freedom, and the deep cause of death, because it is separation from God, the source of life *(See Rom. 5:12)*, and then, in its turn, the occasion and effect of an intervention in us and in our world of an obscure agent, the Devil. Evil is not merely a lack of something, but an effective agent, a living, spiritual being, perverted and perverting. A terrible reality. Mysterious and frightening.

Problem of Evil

It is contrary to the teaching of the Bible and the Church to refuse to recognize the existence of such a reality, or regard it as a principle in itself which does not draw its origin from God like every other creature; or to explain it as a pseudo-reality, a conceptual and fanciful personification of the unknown causes of our misfortunes. The problem of evil, seen in its complexity, and in its absurdity from the viewpoint of our one-sided rationality, becomes an obsession. It is the greatest difficulty for our religious understanding of the cosmos. Not for nothing did St. Augustine suffer over it for years: "Quaerebam unde malum, et non erat exitus," I sought the origin of evil, and I found no explanation. (*Confess.* VII, 5, 7, 11, etc.; *PL* 32, 736, 739).

Here, then, is the importance of the recognition of evil for our correct Christian understanding of the world, life and salvation. First, in the unfolding of evangelical history at the beginning of Christ's public life: who does not remember the account, pregnant with meaning, of His threefold temptation? Then in the many episodes of the Gospel, in which the Devil crosses the path of the Lord and figures in His teaching? (e.g. *Matt.* 12:43). And how could we forget that Christ, referring three times to the Devil, as His adversary, calls him "prince of the world" (*See Jn.* 12:31; 14:30; 16:11)? This overhanging fateful presence is mentioned in many passages of the new Testament. St. Paul calls him "the god of this world." (*See 2 Cor.* 4:4). He warns us of the struggle in the dark that we Christians must wage not against one Devil only, but against many of them: "Put on the whole armour of God, the Apostle says, that you may be able to stand against the wiles of the devil. For we are not contending against flesh and blood, but against the principalities, against the powers, against the world rulers of this present darkness, against the spiritual hosts of wickedness in the heavenly places." (*Eph.* 6:11-12).

That it is not a question of one Devil, but of many, is indicated by various passages in the Gospel. (*See Lk.* 11:21; *Mk.* 5:9). But the principal one is Satan, which means the adversary, the enemy; and with him many, all creatures of God, but fallen, because of their rebellion and damnation (*Cf. Denz.-Sch.* 800-428); a whole mysterious world, upset by an unhappy drama, of which we know very little.

Hidden Enemy Who Sows Errors

We know many things, however, about this diabolical world, which concern our life and the whole history of man. The Devil is at the origin of the first misfortune of mankind; he was the cunning and fatal tempter of the first sin, original sin. (*See Gen.* 3; *Wis.* 1:24). From that fall of Adam the Devil acquired a certain dominion over man, from which only Christ's Redemption can save us. It is a story that is still going on: let us recall the exorcisms of baptism and the frequent references of Holy Scripture and the liturgy to the aggressive and oppressive "powers of darkness" (*Cf. Lk.* 22:53, *Col.* 1:13). He is the enemy number one, the tempter par excellence.

So we know that this dark and disturbing Spirit really exists, and that he still acts with treacherous cunning; he is the secret enemy that sows errors and misfortunes in human history. We should recall the revealing evangelical parable of the wheat and the weeds, the synthesis and explanation of the illogicality that seems to preside over our conflicting vicissitudes: "inimicus homo hoc fecit." (*See Matt* 13:28). He was "a murderer from the beginning...and the father of lies," as Christ defines him (*See Jn.* 8:44-45); he launches sophistic attacks on the moral equilibrium of man. He is the treacherous and cunning enchanter, who finds his way into us by way of the senses, the imagination, lust, utopian logic, or disorderly social contacts in the give and take of life, to introduce deviations, as harmful as they are apparently in conformity with our physical or psychical structures, or our deep, instinctive aspirations.

Catholic Doctrine

This question of the Devil and the influence he can exert on individual persons as well as on communities, whole societies or events, is a very important chapter of Catholic doctrine which is given little attention today, though it should be studied again. Some people think a sufficient compensation can be found in psycho-analytical and psychiatric studies or in spiritualistic experiences, so widespread, unfortunately, in some countries today. People are afraid of falling into old

Manichean theories again, or into frightening divagations of fancy and superstition. Today people prefer to appear strong and unprejudiced, to pose as positivists, while at the same time giving credit to so many unwarranted magical or popular superstitions, or, worse still, opening their souls—their own baptized souls, visited so often by the eucharistic presence and inhabited by the Holy Spirit!—to the licentious experiences of the sense, and to the harmful ones of drugs, as well as to the ideological seductions of fashionable errors, cracks, through which the Devil can easily penetrate and work upon the human mind. Not that every sin is directly due to diabolical action (*Cf. S. Th.* 1, 104, 3); but it is true that those who do not watch over themselves with a certain moral strictness (*Cf. Matt.* 12:45; *Eph.* 6:11) are exposed to the influence of the "mysterium iniquitatis," to which St. Paul refers (*See 2 Thess.* 2:3-12), and run the risk of being damned.

Our doctrine becomes uncertain, obscured as it is by the darkness surrounding the Devil. But our curiosity, excited by the certainty of his multiple existence, justifies two questions. Are there signs, and what are they, of the presence of diabolical action? And what are the means of defense against such an insidious danger?

Presence of the Action of the Devil

We must be very cautious in answering the first question, even if the signs of the Evil One sometimes seem evident (*Cf.* Tertullian, *Apol.* 23). We can assume his sinister action where denial of God becomes radical, subtle and absurd, where hypocritical and blatant lies assert themselves against evident truth, where love is extinguished by cold, cruel selfishness, where the name of Christ is impugned with wilfull and rebellious hatred (*Cf. 1 Cor.* 16:22; 12:3), where the spirit of the Gospel is watered down and denied, where despair has the last word, etc. But it is too wide and difficult a diagnosis for us to attempt to study and authenticate it now. For everyone, however, it has a dramatic interest, to which even modern literature bears witness (*Cf.* e.g. the works of Bernanos, studied by Ch. Moeller, *Littér. du XX siécle*, I, p. 397 ss.; P. Macchi, *II volto del male in Bernanos;* cf. also *Satan, Etudes Carmélitaines*, Desclée de Br., 1948). The problem of evil remains one of the greatest and permanent problems for the human spirit, even after the victorious answer given by Jesus Christ. "We know that we are of God," the Evangelist St. John writes, "but the whole world is in the power of the evil one." *(1 Jn.* 5:19).

The Christian's Defense

To the other question: what defense, what remedy is there against the action of the Devil, the answer is easier, even if it remains difficult to carry out. We could say: everything that defends us from sin shelters us for that very reason from the invisible enemy. Grace is the decisive defense. Innocence takes on the aspect of a fortress. Everyone remembers how often apostolic teaching symbolized, in the armour of a soldier, the virtues that can make the Christian invulnerable. *(Cf. Rom.* 13:12; *Eph.* 6:11, 14, 17; *1 Thess.* 5:8). The Christian must be militant; he must be vigilant and strong *(See 1 Ptr.* 5:8); and he must sometimes have recourse to some special ascetic exercises to stave off certain diabolical attacks. Jesus teaches this, indicating "prayer and fasting" as the remedy. *(See Mk.* 9:29). The Apostle suggests the main line to follow: "Resist evil and conquer it with good." *(Rom.* 12:21; *Matt.* 13:29).

With the awareness therefore, of the present adversities in which souls, the Church, the world find themselves today, we will try to give meaning and efficacy to the usual invocation of our principal prayer: "Our Father. . .deliver us from evil!"

Let our Apostolic Blessing serve this purpose too.

EXORCISM

Against Satan and the Rebellious Angels

Published by order of His Holiness, Pope Leo XIII.

The Holy Father exhorts priests to say this prayer as often as possible, as a simple exorcism to curb the power of the devil and prevent him from doing harm. The faithful also may say it in their own name for the same purpose, as any approved prayer. Its use is recommended whenever action of the devil is suspected, causing malice in men, violent temptations, and even storms and various calamities. It could be used as a solemn exorcism (an official and public ceremony, in Latin) to expel the devil. It would then be said by a priest, in the name of the Church, and only with the Bishop's permission.

In the Name of the Father and of the Son and of the Holy Ghost. Amen.

Prayer to St. Michael the Archangel

Glorious Prince of the Celestial Host, St. Michael the Archangel, defend us in the conflict which we have to sustain "against principalities and powers, against the rulers of the world of this darkness, against the spirits of wickedness in the high places." *(Ephes. 6:12).* Come to the rescue of men, whom God has created to His image and likeness, and whom He has redeemed at a great price from the tyranny of the devil. It is thou whom Holy Church venerates as her guardian and her protector, thou whom the Lord has charged to conduct redeemed souls into

Heaven. Pray, therefore, the God of Peace to subdue Satan beneath our feet, that he may no longer retain men captive nor do injury to the Church. Present our prayers to the Most High, that without delay they may draw His mercy down upon us. Seize "the dragon, the old serpent, which is the devil and Satan," bind him and cast him into the bottomless pit ". . . that he (may) no more seduce the nations." (*Apoc.* 20:2-3).

Exorcism

In the Name of Jesus Christ, Our Lord and Saviour, strengthened by the intercession of the Immaculate Virgin Mary, Mother of God, of Blessed Michael the Archangel, of the Blessed Apostles Peter and Paul, and all the Saints, and powerful in the holy authority of our ministry, we confidently undertake to repulse the attack and deceits of the devil.

Let God arise, and let His enemies be scattered: and let them that hate Him flee from before His face.

"As smoke vanisheth, so let them vanish away: as wax melteth before the fire, so let the wicked perish at the presence of God." (*Psalm* 67:2-3).

V. Behold the Cross of the Lord! Flee, bands of enemies.
R. The Lion of the Tribe of Juda, the Offspring of David, hath conquered.
V. May Thy mercy descend upon us.
R. As great as our hope in Thee.

We drive you from us, whoever you may be, unclean spirits, Satanic powers, infernal invaders, wicked legions, assemblies and sects. In the name and by the virtue of Our Lord Jesus Christ ✠, may you be snatched away and driven from the Church of God and from the souls redeemed by the Precious Blood of the Divine Lamb ✠. Cease by your audacity, cunning serpent, to delude the human race, to persecute the Church, to torment God's elect, and to sift them as wheat ✠. This is the command made to you by the most High God ✠, with Whom in your haughty insolence you still pretend to be equal ✠, the God "Who will have all men to be saved, and to come to the knowledge of the truth." (*I Tim.* 2:4). God the Father commands you ✠; God the Son commands you ✠;

God the Holy Ghost commands you ✠. Christ commands you, the Eternal Word of God made Flesh; He Who to have our race, out-done through your malice, "humbled Himself, becoming obedient unto death." *(Phil. 2:8)*; He Who has built His Church on the firm rock and declared that the gates of Hell shall not prevail against her, because He dwells with her "all days, even to the consummation of the world." *(Matt. 28:20)*. The hidden virtue of the Cross requires it of you as does also the power of the mysteries of the Christian Faith ✠. The glorious Mother of God, the Virgin Mary, commands you ✠; she who by her humility and from the first moment of her Immaculate Conception crushed your proud head. The faith of the holy Apostles Peter and Paul and of the other Apostles commands you ✠. The blood of the martyrs and the pious intercession of all the Saints command you ✠.

Thus, cursed dragon, and you, wicked legions, we adjure you by the living God ✠, by the true God ✠, by the Holy God ✠, by the God Who "so loved the world, as to give His only-begotten Son; that whosoever believeth in Him, may not perish but may have life everlasting." *(Jn. 3:16)*: Cease deceiving human creatures and pouring out to them the poison of eternal perdition; cease harming the Church and hindering her liberty. Retreat, Satan, inventor and master of all deceit, enemy of man's salvation. Cede the place to Christ in Whom you have found none of your works. Cede the place to the One, Holy, Catholic, and Apostolic Church acquired by Christ at the price of His Blood. Stoop beneath the all-powerful Hand of God, tremble and flee at the evocation of the holy and terrible Name of Jesus, this Name which causes Hell to tremble, this name to which the Virtues, Powers, and Dominations of Heaven are humbly submissive, this name which the Cherubim and Seraphim praise unceasingly, repeating: Holy, Holy, Holy is the Lord, the God of hosts.

V. O Lord, hear my prayer.
R. And let my cry come unto Thee.

V. May the Lord be with thee.
R. And with thy spirit.

Let Us Pray

God of Heaven, God of earth, God of Angels, God of Archangels, God of Patriarchs, God of Prophets, God of Apostles, God of Martyrs, God of Confessors, God of Virgins, God Who hast power to give life after death and rest after work, because there is no other God than Thee and there can be no other, for Thou art the Creator of all things, visible and invisible, of Whose reign there shall be no end, we humbly prostrate ourselves before Thy glorious majesty and we supplicate Thee to deliver us from all the tyranny of the infernal spirits, from their snares, and their furious wickedness. Deign, O Lord, to protect us by Thy power and to preserve us safe and sound. We beseech Thee through Jesus Christ Our Lord. Amen.

From the snares of the devil, deliver us, O Lord.

That Thy Church may serve Thee in peace and liberty, We beseech Thee to hear us.

That Thou wouldst crush down all enemies of Thy Church, We beseech Thee to hear us.

(Holy Water is sprinkled in the place where we may be.)

IMPRIMATUR: Manuel, Bishop of Barcelona
December 19, 1931

Prayer to St. Michael

Composed by Pope Leo XIII (1878-1903) and formerly said after low Mass in Catholic churches.

Saint Michael, the Archangel, defend us in battle; be our defense against the wickedness and snares of the devil. May God rebuke him, we humbly pray; and do thou, O Prince of the heavenly host; by the power of God, thrust into Hell Satan and the other evil spirits who prowl about the world for the ruin of souls. Amen.

NIHIL OBSTAT: John A. Goodwine, J.C.D.
Censor Librorum

IMPRIMATUR: Francis Cardinal Spellman
Archbishop of New York
February 24, 1961

MESSAGE OF MARY'S MATERNAL LOVE

Pope John Paul's Homily at Mass in Fatima on May 13, 1982.

On Thursday, May 13, 1982, the second day of Pope John Paul's pilgrimage to Portugal, the Holy Father visited Fatima to commemorate in a very special way the first anniversary of the attempt on his life and the sixty-fifth anniversary of Our Lady's first apparition at Fatima. During the Mass at the Shrine, the Holy Father delivered the following homily.

1. "And from that hour the disciple took her to his own home."
   (*Jn.* 19:27).

   These are the concluding words of the Gospel in today's liturgy at Fatima. The disciple's name was John. It was he, the son of Zebedee, the apostle and evangelist, who heard from the Cross the words of Christ: "Behold, your mother." But first Christ had said to His Mother: "Woman, behold your son."

   This was a wonderful testament.

   As He left this world, Christ gave to His Mother a man, a human being, to be like a son for her: John. He entrusted him to her. And, as a consequence of this giving and entrusting, Mary became the mother of John. The Mother of God became the Mother of man.

   From that hour John, "took her to his own home" and became the earthly guardian of the Mother of His Master; for sons have the right and duty to care for their mother.

John became by Christ's will the son of the Mother of God. And in John every human being became her child.

The Mother's Presence

2. The words "he took her to his own home" can be taken in the literal sense as referring to the place where he lived.

Mary's motherhood in our regard is manifested in a particular way in the places where she meets us: her dwelling places; places in which a special presence of the Mother is felt.

There are many such dwelling places. They are of all kinds: from a special corner in the home or little wayside shrines adorned with an image of the Mother of God, to chapels and churches built in her honor. However, in certain places the Mother's presence is felt in a particularly vivid way. These places sometimes radiate their light over a great distance and draw people from afar. Their radiance may extend over a diocese, a whole nation, or at times over several countries and even continents. These places are **the Marian sanctuaries or shrines.**

In all these places that unique testament of the Crucified Lord is wonderfully actualized: in them man feels that he is entrusted and confided to Mary; he goes there in order to be with her, as with his Mother; he opens his heart to her and speaks to her about everything; he "takes her to his own home," that is to say, he brings her into all his problems, which at times are difficult. His own problems and those of others. The problems of the family, of societies, of nations, and of the whole of humanity.

Through God's Mercy

3. Is this not the case with the shrine at Lourdes, in France? Is not this the case with Jasna Gora, in Poland, my own country's shrine, which this year is celebrating its six hundredth anniversary?

There too, as in so many other shrines of Mary throughout the world, the words of today's liturgy seem to resound with a particular authentic force: "You are the great pride of our nation" (*Jdth.* 15:9), and also: "...when our nation was brought low. . .you avenged our ruin, walking in the straight path before our God." *(Jdth.* 13:20).

At Fatima these words resound as one particular echo of the experiences not only of the *Portuguese nation* but also of so many other countries and peoples on this earth: indeed, they echo the experience of *modern mankind as a whole,* the whole of the human family.

4. And so I come here today because on this very day last year, in Saint Peter's Square in Rome, the attempt on the Pope's life was made, in mysterious coincidence with the anniversary of the first apparition at Fatima, which occurred on May 13, 1917.

I seemed to recognize in the coincidence of the dates a special call to come to this place. And so, today I am here. I have come in order to thank Divine Providence in this place which the Mother of God seems to have chosen in a particular way. *Misericordiae Domini, qui a non sumus consumpti (Through* God's mercy we were spared—*Lam.* 3:22), I repeat once more with the prophet.

I have come especially in order to confess here the glory of God Himself:

"Blessed be the Lord God, who created the heavens and the earth," I say in the words of today's liturgy. *(Jdth.* 13:18).

And to the Creator of Heaven and earth I also raise that special hymn of glory which is she herself, **the Immaculate Mother of the Incarnate Word**.

"O daughter, you are blessed by the Most High God above all women on earth. . .your hope will never depart from the hearts of men, as they remember the power of God. May God grant this to be a perpetual honor to you." *(Jdth.* 18:20).

At *the basis of this song* of praise which the Church lifts up with joy here as in so many other places on the earth, is the incomparable choice of a daughter of the human race to be the Mother of God.

And therefore let God above all be praised: Father, Son and Holy Spirit.

May blessing and veneration be given to Mary, the model of the Church, as the **"dwelling-place of the Most Holy Trinity."**

Spiritual Motherhood

5. From the time when Jesus, dying on the Cross, said to John: "Behold, your mother"; from the time when "the disciple took her to his own home," the mystery of the spiritual motherhood of Mary has been actualized boundlessly in history. Motherhood means caring for the life of the child. Since Mary is the mother of us all, her care for the life of man is universal. The care of a mother embraces her child totally. Mary's motherhood has its beginning in her motherly care for Christ. In Christ, at the foot of the Cross, she accepted John, and in John she accepted all of us totally. Mary embraces us all with special solicitude in the Holy Spirit. For as we profess in our Creed, He is "the giver of life." It is He Who gives the fullness of life, open towards eternity.

   Mary's spiritual motherhood is therefore a sharing in the power of the Holy Spirit, of "the giver of life." It is the humble service of her who says of herself: "Behold, I am the handmaid of the Lord." (*Lk.* 1:38).

   In the light of the mystery of Mary's spiritual motherhood, let us seek to understand the extraordinary message, which began on May 13, 1917 to resound throughout the world from Fatima, continuing for five months until October 13th of the same year.

Convert and Repent

6. The Church as always taught and continues to proclaim that God's revelation was brought to completion in Jesus Christ, Who is the fullness of that revelation, and that "no new public revelation is to be expected before the glorious manifestation of Our Lord." (*Dei Verbum,* 4). The Church evaluates and judges private revelations by the criterion of conformity with that single public Revelation.

   If the Church has accepted the message of Fatima, it is above all because that message contains a truth and a call whose basic content is **the truth and the call of the Gospel** itself.

   "Repent, and believe in the gospel" (*Mk.* 1:15): these are the first words that the Messiah addressed to humanity. The message of Fatima is, in its basic nucleus, a call to conversion and repentance, as in the Gospel. This call was uttered at the beginning of the twentieth century, and it was thus addressed particularly to this present century. The Lady of the message seems to have read with special insight the "signs of the times," the signs of our time.

The call to repentance is a motherly one, and at the same time it is strong and decisive. The love that "rejoices in the truth" (*Cf. 1 Cor.* 13) is capable of being clear-cut and firm. The call to repentance is linked, as always, with a call to prayer. In harmony with the tradition of many centuries, the Lady of the message indicates the **Rosary**, which can rightly be defined as "Mary's prayer": the prayer in which she feels particularly united with us. She herself prays with us. **The Rosary prayer** embraces the problems of the Church, of the See of Saint Peter, the problems of the whole world. In it we also remember sinners, that they may be converted and saved, and the souls in Purgatory.

The words of the message were addressed to children aged from seven to ten. Children, like Bernadette of Lourdes, are particularly privileged in the apparitions of the Mother of God. Hence the fact that also her language is simple, within the limits of their understanding. The children of Fatima became partners in dialogue with the Lady of the message and collaborators with her. One of them is still living.

Recommends the Rosary

7. When Jesus on the Cross said "Woman, behold your son" (*Jn.* 19:26), in a new way He opened His Mother's Heart, the Immaculate Heart, and revealed to it the new dimensions and extent of the love to which she was called in the Holy Spirit by the power of the sacrifice of the Cross.

In the words of Fatima we seem to find this dimension of motherly love, whose range covers the whole of man's path towards God; the path that leads through this world and that goes, through Purgatory, beyond this world. The solicitude of the Mother of the Saviour is solicitude for the work of salvation; the work of her Son. It is solicitude for the salvation, the eternal salvation, of all. Now that sixty-five years have passed since May 13, 1917, it is difficult to fail to notice how the range of this salvific love of the Mother embraces, in a particular way, our century.

In the light of a mother's love we understand the whole message of the Lady of Fatima. The greatest obstacle to man's journey towards God is sin, perseverance in sin, and, finally, denial of God. The deliberate blotting out of God from the world of human thought. The detachment from Him of the whole of man's earthly activity. The rejection of God by man.

In reality, the eternal salvation of man is only in God. Man's rejection of God, if it becomes definitive, leads logically to God's rejection of man (*Cf. Matt.* 7:23; 10:33), to damnation.

Can the Mother who with all the force of the love that she fosters in the Holy Spirit desires everyone's salvation keep silence on what undermines the very bases of their salvation? No, she cannot.

And so, while the message of Our Lady of Fatima is a motherly one, it is also strong and decisive. It sounds severe. It sounds like John the Baptist speaking on the banks of the Jordan. It invites to repentance. It gives a warning. It calls to prayer. It recommends the Rosary.

The message is addressed to every human being. The love of the Saviour's Mother reaches every place touched by the work of salvation. Her care extends to every individual of our time, and to all the societies, nations and peoples. Societies menaced by apostasy, threatened by moral degradation. The collapse of morality involves the collapse of societies.

Meaning of Consecration

8. On the Cross Christ said: "Woman, behold, your son!" With these words He opened in a new way His Mother's heart. A little later, the Roman soldier's spear pierced the side of the Crucified One. That pierced heart became a sign of the redemption achieved through the death of the Lamb of God.

The Immaculate Heart of Mary, opened with the words

"Woman, behold, your son!", is spiritually united with the heart of her Son opened by the soldier's spear. Mary's Heart was opened by the same love for man and for the world with which Christ loved man and the world, offering Himself for them on the Cross, until the soldier's spear struck that blow.

Consecrating the world to the Immaculate Heart of Mary means drawing near, through the Mother's intercession, to the very Fountain of life that sprang from Golgotha. This Fountain pours forth unceasingly redemption and grace. In it reparation is made continually for the sins of the world. It is a ceaseless source of new life and holiness.

Consecrating the world to the Immaculate Heart of the Mother means returning beneath the Cross of the Son. It means consecrating this world to the pierced Heart of the Saviour, bringing it back to the very source of its Redemption. Redemption is always greater than man's sin and the "sin of the world." The power of the Redemption is infinitely superior to the whole range of evil in man and the world.

The Heart of the Mother is aware of this, more than any other heart in the whole universe, visible and invisible.

And so she calls us. She not only calls us to be converted: she calls us to accept her motherly help to return to the source of Redemption.

Love For All Persons

9. Consecrating ourselves to Mary means accepting her help to offer ourselves and the whole of mankind to Him Who is Holy, infinitely Holy; it means accepting her help—by having recourse to her Motherly Heart, which beneath the Cross was opened to love for every human being, for the whole world—in order to offer the world, the individual human being, mankind as a whole, and all the nations to Him Who is infinitely Holy. God's holiness showed itself in the redemption of man, of the world, of the whole of mankind, and of the nations: a redemption brought about through the Sacrifice of the Cross. "For their sake I consecrate myself," Jesus had said. (*Jn.* 17:19).

By the power of the redemption the world and man
have been consecrated. They have been consecrated to Him
who is infinitely Holy. They have been offered and entrusted to Love itself, merciful Love.

The Mother of Christ calls us, invites us to join with
the Church of the living God in the consecration of the
world, in this act of confiding by which the world, mankind as a whole, the nations, and each individual person
are presented to the Eternal Father with the power of the
Redemption won by Christ. They are offered in the Heart
of the Redeemer which was pierced on the Cross.

Rooted in the Gospel

10. The appeal of the Lady of the message of Fatima is so
deeply rooted in the Gospel and the whole of Tradition
that the **Church feels that the message imposes a commitment on her**.

She has responded through the Servant of God Pius
XII (whose episcopal ordination took place precisely on
May 13, 1917): he consecrated the human race and espe-
cially the Peoples of Russia to the Immaculate Heart of
Mary. Was not that consecration his response to the evan-
gelical eloquence of the call of Fatima?

In its Dogmatic Constitution on the Church *(Lumen Gentium)* and its Pastoral Constitution on the Church in the
Modern World *(Gaudium et Spes)* the Second Vatican Council amply illustrated the reasons for the link between the
Church and the world of today. Furthermore, its teaching
on Mary's special place in the mystery of Christ and the
Church bore mature fruit in Paul VI's action in calling
Mary Mother of the Church and thus indicating more
profoundly the nature of her care for the world, for mankind, for each human being, and for all the nations: what
characterizes them is her motherhood.

This brought a further deepening of understanding of
the meaning of the act of consecrating that the Church
is called upon to perform with the help of the Heart of
Christ's Mother and ours.

Many Going Astray

11. Today John Paul II, successor of Peter, continuer of the work of Pius, John, and Paul, and particular heir of the Second Vatican Council, presents himself before the Mother of the Son of God in her Shrine at Fatima. In what way does he come?

He presents himself, reading again with trepidation the motherly call to penance, to conversion, the ardent appeal of the Heart of Mary that resounded at Fatima sixty-five years ago. Yes, he reads it again with trepidation in his heart, because he sees how so many people and societies—how many Christians—have gone in the opposite direction to the one indicated in the message of Fatima. Sin has thus made itself firmly at home in the world, and denial of God has become widespread in the ideologies, ideas and plans of human beings.

But for this very reason the evangelical call to repentance and conversion, uttered in the Mother's message, remains ever relevant. It is still more relevant than it was sixty-five years ago. It is still more urgent. And so it is to be the subject of next year's Synod of Bishops, which we are already preparing for.

The successor of Peter presents himself here also as a witness to the immensity of human suffering, a witness to the almost apocalyptic menaces looking over the nations and mankind as a whole. He is trying to embrace these sufferings with his own weak human heart, as he places himself before the mystery of the Heart of the Mother, the Immaculate Heart of Mary.

In the name of these sufferings and with awareness of the evil that is spreading throughout the world and menacing the individual human being, the nations, and mankind as a whole, Peter's successor presents himself here with greater faith in the redemption of the world, in the saving Love that is always stronger, always more powerful than any evil.

My heart is oppressed when I see the sin of the world and the whole range of menaces gathering like a dark cloud over mankind, but it also rejoices with hope as I once more do what has been done by my Predecessors, when they consecrated the world to the Heart of the Mother, when they consecrated especially to that Heart those peoples which particularly need to be consecrated. Doing this means consecrating the world to Him Who is infinite Holiness. This Holiness means redemption. It means a love more powerful than evil. No "sin of the world" can ever overcome this Love.

Once more this act is being done. Mary's appeal is not just for once. Her appeal must be taken up by generation after generation, in accordance with the every new "signs of the times." It must be unceasingly returned to. It must ever be taken up anew.

Faith of the Church

12. The author of the Apocalypse wrote: "And I saw the holy city, new Jerusalem, coming down out of heaven from God, prepared as a bride adorned for her husband; and I heard a loud voice from the throne saying, "Behold, the dwelling of God is with men. He will dwell with them, and they shall be his people, and God himself will be with them." (*Rev.* 21:2-3).

This is the faith by which the Church lives. This is the faith with which the People of God makes its journey.

"The dwelling of God is with men" on earth even now. In that dwelling is the Heart of the Bride and Mother, Mary, a Heart adorned with the jewel of her Immaculate Conception. The Heart of the Bride and Mother which was opened beneath the Cross by the word of her Son to a great new love for man and the world. The Heart of the Bride and Mother which is aware of all the sufferings of individuals and societies on earth.

The People of God is a pilgrim along the ways of this world in an eschatological direction. It is making its pilgrimage towards the eternal Jerusalem, towards "the dwelling of God with men." God will there "wipe away every tear from their eyes, and death shall be no more, neither shall there be mourning nor crying nor pain any more, for the former things have passed away."

But at present "the former things" are still in existence. They it is that constitute the temporal setting of our pilgrimage.

For that reason we look towards "Him who sits upon the throne and say, 'Behold, I make all things new'" (*Rev.* 21:5).

And together with the Evangelist and Apostle we try to see with the eyes of faith "the new heaven and the new earth"; for the first heaven and the first earth have passed away.

But "the first heaven and the first earth" still exist around and within us. We cannot ignore it. But this enables us to recognize what an immense grace was granted to us human beings when, in the midst of our pilgrimage, there shone forth on the horizon of the faith of our times this "great portent, a woman." (*Cf. Rev.* 12:1).

Yes, truly we can repeat: "O daughter, you are blessed by the Most High God above all women on earth... walking in the straight path before our God... **you have avenged our ruin." Truly indeed, you are blessed.**

Yes, here and throughout the Church, in the heart of every individual and in the world as a whole, may you be blessed, O Mary, our sweet Mother.

Appendix D

THE RATZINGER REPORT

An in-depth interview of Joseph Cardinal Ratzinger, by Vittorio Messori, concerning the State of the Church, resulted in the highly acclaimed book, THE RATZINGER REPORT (Ignatius Press).

Chapter 10 of the book presents Cardinal Ratzinger's thoughts on Satan. Not surprisingly, his thoughts mirror those of Pope Paul VI, and more currently, those of Pope John Paul II.

On November 15, 1972, Pope Paul VI delivered his often quoted speech regarding Satan. At that time he stated: "I have the feeling that the smoke of Satan has penetrated the Temple of God." He went on to say: "I believe in something supernatural that has come into the world to destroy and strangle the very fruits of the Ecumenical Council and to stop the Church from breaking out into a hymn of joy, by sowing doubt, uncertainty, problems, unrest and discontent."

He went on to say that "the evil which exists in the world is the result and effect of an attack upon us and our society by a dark and hostile agent, the devil." The Holy Father confirmed the Church's teaching and belief in the existence of Satan. At the same time he confirmed that many people refuse to acknowledge his existence, or explain him away as a pseudo-reality. He finished up by stating: "The devil is the enemy number one, the source of all temptation. Thus we know that this dark and destructive being really exists and is still active."

Cardinal Ratzinger, the Prefect of the Congregation for the Faith, strongly attests to the words of the former Pontiff.

In 1975, The Congregation for the Faith issued a document on the subject. It stated: "The teaching concerning the devil is an undisputed element of the Christian awareness," and that, "it is based on its greatest source, namely, the teaching of Christ."

Although many liberal scholars are under the misconception that Vatican II took an opposite position, they should take note the Church's traditional teaching on Satan, ratified by Vatican II, speaks seventeen times of "Satan," using that name specifically, or one of his other recognizable titles.

In the RATZINGER REPORT, the Cardinal re-affirms the Church's Doctrine:

"Whatever the less discerning theologians may say, the devil, as far as Christian belief is concerned, is a puzzling but real, personal and not merely symbolical presence. He is a powerful reality, the 'prince of this world,' as he is called by the New Testament, which continually reminds us of his existence. This is evident if we look realistically at history, with its abyss of ever new atrocities which cannot be explained by reference to man alone. On his own, man has not the power to oppose Satan, but the devil is not a second God, and united with Jesus we can be certain of vanquishing him."

The prefect went on to say: "If this redeeming light of Christianity were to fail, the world with all its knowledge and technology would slip back into an inescapable fear in the face of the alien impenetrability of being. There are already signs of the return of these dark powers, and Satanic cults are spreading more and more in the secularized world."

As would be expected, many scoffed at Pope Paul's hardline position of fifteen years ago. The reality of his words are now upon us. Many also scoffed at Cardinal Ratzinger's prediction. The rise in Satanic activity is now surfacing everywhere, and those knowledgeable, recognize it is only the tip of the iceberg. Its current alluring form of enticement comes to us in the form of "New Age Religion."

APPENDIX E

OFFICE OF READINGS, WEDNESDAY, FIRST WEEK OF ADVENT

(From a sermon by Saint Bernard, abbot.)

"We know that there are three comings of the Lord. The third lies between the other two. It is invisible, while the other two are visible. In the first coming He was seen on earth, dwelling among men; He Himself testifies that they saw Him and hated Him. In the final coming *all flesh will see the salvation of our God,* and *they will look on Him Whom they pierced.* The intermediate coming is a hidden one; in it only the elect see the Lord within their own selves, and they are saved. In His first coming our Lord came in our flesh and in our weakness; in this middle coming He comes in spirit and in power; in the final coming He will be seen in glory and majesty.

"Because this coming lies between the other two, it is like a road on which we travel from the first coming to the last. In the first, Christ was our redemption; in the last, He will appear as our life; in this middle coming, He is our rest and consolation.

"In case someone should think that what we say about this middle coming is sheer invention, listen to what our Lord Himself says: *If anyone loves me, he will keep my word, and my Father will love him, and we will come to him.* There is another passage of Scripture which reads: *He who fears God will do good,* but something further has been said about the one who loves us, that is, that he will keep God's word. Where is God's word to be kept? Obviously in the heart,

143

as the prophet says: *I have hidden your words in my heart,
so that I may not sin against you.*

"Keep God's word in this way. Let it enter into your very
being, let it take possession of your desires and your whole
way of life. Feed on goodness, and your soul will delight in
its richness. Remember to eat your bread, or your heart will
wither away. Fill your soul with richness and strength.

"If you keep the word of God in this way, it will also keep
you. The Son with the Father will come to you. The great
Prophet Who will build the new Jerusalem will come, the
One Who makes all things new. This coming will fulfill what
is written: *As we have borne the likeness of the earthly man,
we shall also bear the likeness of the heavenly man.* Just as
Adam's sin spread through all mankind and took hold of
all, so Christ, Who created and redeemed all, will glorify
all, once He takes possesion of all."

AFTERWORD

This book has attempted to provide the reader with Biblical and Church Doctrine relating to the existence of Satan. We have tried to show evidence of his reality through example of the how, what, where and why of some of his attempts to detour our pilgrimage to salvation.

We have also attempted to show the Scripture background and reference to this reality. It is a reality that has somehow been pushed into the dark corners of our lives. The reality seems to have vanished—along with sin. In looking the world square in the eye today, do you really think sin has vanished?

We have also attempted to provide examples of Satan's reality as it relates to our everyday lives, and the lives of the Church proper. There is one aspect however, that we did not touch on, simply because of the size and scope of its dreadful existence. And that is the subject of "New Age Religion."

This currently "hot topic" comes to us under many intricate and obscure forms, all of which pretend to be good. (So was the temptation of Adam and Eve, in the Book of Genesis.) However, the bottom line with all of these new movements is that they attempt to make us God, and eliminate the need for God.

The bottom line is also very simple. If you are not serving the Lord, then you are serving His adversary. There is no other way, no other explanation. This entire new age syndrome needs to be addressed in a separate book, and because of the urgent need for all of us to become knowledgeable regarding this attempt by Satan to undermine the Christian world with this new religion, we are suggesting several existing titles that address this issue in depth. They can be ac-

145

quired from the publisher of this book, FAITH PUBLISHING COMPANY.

THE UNICORN IN THE SANCTUARY, by Randy England. The impact of the new age on the Catholic Church. 168 pgs.

A CRISIS OF TRUTH, by Ralph Martin. The attack on Faith, Morality, and Mission of the Catholic Church. 250 pgs.

INSIDE THE NEW AGE NIGHTMARE, by Randall Baer. A former, top New Age leader tells his story. 200 pgs.

CULTS, SECTS, AND THE NEW AGE, by Rev. James LeBar. 288 pgs.

FAITH PUBLISHING COMPANY

Faith Publishing Company has been organized as a service for the publishing and distribution of materials that reflect Christian values, and in particular the teachings of the Catholic Church.

It is dedicated to publication of only those materials that reflect such values.

For further information, or additional copies of this book, contact:

Faith Publishing Company
P.O. Box 237
Milford, Ohio 45150